CUPCAKES
for Kids

50 little cakes for parties, birthdays and special treats

Rosie Anness & Cortina Butler

LORENZ BOOKS

CONTENTS

CUPCAKES
for Kids

We have been making cupcakes together ever since Rosie was a small girl.

Baking these little cakes for birthdays and celebrations or just to entertain ourselves on a wet afternoon was the first proper cooking that she did – standing on a dining chair to reach the kitchen worktop. The quantities were small enough for her to manage the mixing and if something did go wrong the waste was small. The cakes cooked very quickly so there was no time for getting bored while waiting for them to cook and cool down. She loved to dig deep into the box of cupcake cases to find an especially pretty design, and the best task of all was thinking up new combinations of sugar sprinkles, edible glitter and other decorations. She loved to eat cupcakes of course, carefully peeling off the paper case then licking off the icing, but making them was always the greater treat – and still is.

We have given recipes for lots of different cake flavours here combined with different icings. The flavours are all very child friendly and it is fun to go through the recipes with your child and choose a taste that they really like. They are more likely to eat the whole cake that way. But you can always use just plain vanilla bases or mix and match their favourite flavour with another design.

We have also included recipes for a few other types of little cakes. Whoopie pies are pairs of round cakes (a little like soft cookies), sandwiched with a buttercream-style filling, that originated in America. Cake pops are balls of cake coated in chocolate or another covering and presented on a lollipop stick. And we have also given a recipe for colourful miniature macarons, intended for children, but quite hard for adults to resist.

Have fun making and decorating these cakes – there are plenty of simple recipes that your child can make with you. And as for the slightly more complicated designs ... the expression on your child's face when they see a plate of decorated cakes will be worth any effort involved in making them.

Rosie & Cortina

She loved to dig deep into the box of cupcake cases ...

CUPCAKE BASICS

Cakes really are easy to make as long as you have the ingredients at room temperature (this genuinely does make a difference), you measure carefully and your oven is working properly – and even if they're not perfect remember that once iced and decorated they'll look delicious.

CASES

Confusingly, cupcake cases come in different sizes that may all be labelled as 'cupcake' cases. We have used the middle-sized cases, often called standard cupcake cases, that measure about 5cm/2in across the base and 3cm/1¼in high. The larger cases, also called muffin cases, tend to be too big for most children. If you can only get muffin cases you may find that you only use nine or ten cases rather than twelve. There are also smaller cases often called fairy cake cases. If you wish to use these, the mixture will stretch to 14 or 15 cakes – and may need a little more topping.

Some cases are made of baking parchment and if you can find them these will give a more attractive finished result, especially for darker mixtures such as chocolate. The downside is that the cases sometimes peel away from the baked cakes. We like to save pretty patterns on pale backgrounds for pale mixtures like vanilla and lemon, and find that heavily patterned cases work better with simple toppings, and that more complicated decorations look more attractive with plainer cases. If you want the cake inside to be a surprise – because it has been coloured or marbled for example – use foil cases so that the cake will not show through.

As well as regular shapes you can sometimes also find unusual paper cases in the shape of petals, with handles, or cases made of stiffer paper called baking cups. Individual silicone cases are now widely available, in regular shapes, hearts or even in the shape of teacups with handles. These can be reused, and you can either serve the cakes in the cases if you have enough, or remove the cakes and serve them without a case or with a wrapper. We use them for cakes that we will eat at home so that they don't get lost.

TINS (PANS)

It is essential to place paper cupcake cases in a muffin tin for cooking. The paper cases are not strong enough to hold their shape and will open out without the support of the tin. Place individual silicone cases on a strong baking sheet for baking. Silicone cases, whether individual or multiple moulds, should be greased and dusted lightly with flour before you put in the cake mixture. Although they are theoretically non-stick, the cakes turn out more successfully with preparation.

INGREDIENTS

We have used unsalted butter for these recipes but when making the cakes you can use other fats suitable for baking with good results. Sometimes baking fats produce a more liquid mixture, so you may not need to add milk or juice to obtain a dropping consistency. For buttercream icing though you do need to use butter to get the best flavour. The eggs are all medium eggs weighing roughly 50–65g/2–2½oz each. Have all your ingredients at room temperature if possible, even the few spoonfuls of milk to add to the mixture. If necessary soften hard butter for a few seconds in a microwave, but it really does need just a few seconds at medium heat; it is better to soften the butter in stages than end up with melted butter that will not produce such light cakes.

The temperatures given are for a conventional oven. Most of these recipes are cooked at 180°C/350°F/Gas 4. If you have an electric fan oven take the temperature down to about 170°C/340°F and start to check at the earlier point in the cooking time allowed.

VANILLA CUPCAKE BASE

This recipe is the simplest form of cupcake base. If you prefer you can replace the vanilla extract with the finely grated rind of one lemon and the milk with lemon juice.

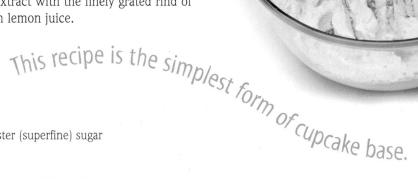

115g/4oz/½ cup butter
115g/4oz/generous ½ cup caster (superfine) sugar
5ml/1 tsp vanilla extract
2 eggs, lightly beaten
115g/4oz/1 cup self-raising (self-rising) flour, sifted
15–30ml/1–2 tbsp milk

▶▶ Makes 12 cupcakes

1 Preheat the oven to 180°C/350°F/Gas 4. Line a muffin tin (pan) with cupcake cases.

2 Cream the butter for a few minutes until soft and pale. Add the sugar and continue to beat until the mixture is pale and fluffy. Add the vanilla extract to the lightly beaten eggs and then gradually add to the butter and sugar mixture, beating well between each addition. Add a teaspoon of flour with the last two additions so that the mixture does not curdle. Fold in the sifted flour and then 15–30ml/1–2 tbsp of milk so that the mixture drops slowly off the spoon.

3 Divide the mixture between the cupcake cases. Bake for 20–25 minutes until risen, lightly browned and bouncy to the touch. Allow to cool in the tin for a few minutes, and then remove and cool on a rack.

CHOCOLATE CUPCAKE BASE

90g/3½oz/¾ cup self-raising (self-rising) flour
25g/1oz/¼ cup unsweetened cocoa powder
115g/4oz/½ cup butter
115g/4oz/scant ¾ cup soft light brown sugar

2 eggs, lightly beaten
15–30ml/1–2 tbsp milk

▶▶ Makes 12 cupcakes

1 Preheat the oven to 180°C/350°F/Gas 4. Line a muffin tin (pan) with cupcake cases. Sift together the flour and the cocoa and set aside.

2 Cream the butter for a few minutes until soft and pale. Add the sugar and continue to beat until the mixture is pale and fluffy. Gradually add the lightly beaten eggs to the butter and sugar mixture, beating well between each addition. Add a teaspoonful of flour with each of the last two additions so that the mixture does not curdle. Fold in the sifted flour and cocoa and then add the milk, a little at a time, so that the mixture drops slowly off the spoon.

3 Divide the mixture between the cupcake cases. Bake for 20–25 minutes until risen, lightly browned and bouncy to the touch. Allow to cool in the tin for a few minutes, and then remove and cool on a rack.

GLUTEN-FREE BAKING

We have family members who cannot eat gluten (a protein found in wheat and other grains including barley and rye), and we have found that ready-mixed gluten-free flour makes an excellent substitute for regular flour in cake recipes. Add a little more milk than you would with regular flour so that the mixture drops easily off the spoon. Self-raising (self-rising) gluten-free flour is increasingly easy to find, but if you can only find plain (all-purpose) gluten-free flour add 5ml/1tsp gluten-free baking powder for 115g/4oz/1 cup flour. It is important to check; not all baking powders are gluten-free. If your child or a visitor is gluten-intolerant, then we suggest that you bake all the cakes gluten-free. The other children won't notice the difference.

If you cannot find gluten-free flour, here is a simple recipe for a cupcake made with rice flour that can be used as a base. Rice flour is very finely ground rice. The slightly coarser ground rice can also be used if very fine rice flour is not available, but the texture will be a little more grainy.

GLUTEN-FREE VANILLA CUPCAKE

115g/4oz/⅔ cup rice flour
5ml/1 tsp gluten-free baking powder
115g/4oz/½ cup butter
115g/4oz/generous ½ cup caster (superfine) sugar
5ml/1 tsp vanilla extract

2 eggs, lightly beaten
15–45ml/1–3 tbsp milk

➡➡ **Makes 12 cupcakes**

1 Preheat the oven to 190°C/375°F/Gas 5. Line a muffin tin (pan) with cupcake cases. Sift the rice flour with the baking powder.

2 Cream the butter for a few minutes until soft and pale. Add the sugar and continue to beat until the mixture is pale and fluffy. Add the vanilla extract to the lightly beaten eggs and then gradually add to the butter and sugar mixture, beating well between each addition. Add a teaspoon of flour with the last two additions so that the mixture does not curdle. Fold in the sifted flour and then 15–45ml/1–3 tbsp of milk so that the mixture drops slowly off the spoon.

3 Divide the mixture between the cupcake cases. Bake for 20–25 minutes until risen, lightly browned and bouncy to the touch. Allow to cool in the tin for a few minutes, and then remove and cool on a rack.

ICINGS

We have used five basic kinds of icing for most of the designs in this book, ready-to-roll fondant icing, glacé icing, buttercream, royal icing and Italian meringue.

READY-TO-ROLL FONDANT ICING

Widely available, ready-to-roll fondant icing is great for modelling 3D designs, or cutting shapes. (This is different from the pourable icing, also called fondant, used to ice little cakes like fondant fancies.) It is possible to get ready-coloured icing but often only in a limited number of colours, and it is easy to colour white icing using gel or paste food colouring – don't try to use liquid colouring. Red, green and black icing are easy to get hold of though, and since it takes a lot of colouring and a lot of kneading to get a good strong colour, it is worth buying these shades ready-coloured if your design requires them. Don't worry if your hands end up brightly coloured too; the colouring easily washes off, though some colours may linger for a few washes.

This sort of icing dries quickly, which is great if you are making shapes to put on a cupcake and don't want to wait too long, but not so good if you forget to cover it and you discover that it has dried hard. Use only what you need and keep the rest of the icing tightly covered with clear film (plastic wrap). Ready-to-roll fondant icing is still edible once it has dried, which makes it good for children's cakes.

Professional cake decorators use a refined version of this icing, sometimes called petal paste or sugar paste, to make flowers and other decorations. It can be obtained from specialist suppliers and rolls out more thinly, shapes better and dries quicker and harder than ready-to-roll fondant. We have used ready-to-roll fondant for these cakes because it is easier to obtain, but if you want a really professional finish then use petal paste.

Don't store cakes with ready-to-roll fondant icing decoration in a sealed plastic box – it seems to make the icing sticky – instead cover loosely with a clean teacloth.

When rolling out ready-to-roll fondant icing we usually dust the board with a little icing (confectioners') sugar. Alternatively you can grease the board with a little white vegetable fat (shortening). This keeps the icing moist and you don't end up with a dusty look.

To make flat shapes, roll the icing out to about 3mm/⅛in thick. It is possible to find lots of different small cutters that make life very easy. You can also cut shapes freehand or make your own template with stiff paper and cut around them with a sharp knife. Set the shapes aside to dry for 5–10 minutes before placing them on the cakes.

GLACÉ ICING

This is the simplest icing of all, just icing (confectioners') sugar mixed with water or juice. It can be coloured with food colouring. It cannot be piped, except for simple lines with a fine round piping nozzle, and has a more translucent finish than royal icing, but it is very quick and delicious, and easy for children to make.

150g/5oz/1¼ cups icing (confectioners') sugar, sifted
30–40ml/2–2½ tbsp water or lemon juice

➡ Makes enough to cover 12 cupcakes

Mix the icing (confectioners') sugar with water or lemon juice just 5ml/1 tsp at a time until thin enough to spread on the cupcake. Be cautious as the icing starts to reach the right consistency. If you are adding liquid colour, start adding it while the icing is still stiff as the colouring will thin it further.

BUTTERCREAM

It wasn't until Rosie started asking for cupcakes like those she had seen in some of the new cake shops that sprang up a few years ago that we started decorating cupcakes with buttercream. The fashion today in cupcake shops is for topping cakes with a phenomenal amount of buttercream – often as much icing above as cake below, and most children do love buttercream topping. But although yummy, it is also very rich, so we have been quite mean with the quantities and most recipes have enough for an attractive layer of piped buttercream rather than a mountain. Buttercream keeps surprisingly well – even without chilling.

115g/4oz/½ cup butter, softened
225g/8oz/2 cups icing (confectioners') sugar, sifted
5ml/1 tsp vanilla extract
5–10ml/1–2 tsp milk

▶▶ **Makes enough to cover 12 cupcakes**

Cream the butter until soft and pale. Gradually add the sifted icing (confectioners') sugar, beating well between each addition. Beat in the vanilla extract and then 5–10ml/1–2 tsp of milk to make the icing just soft enough to pipe. Add the milk to the buttercream cautiously so that it does not become too soft.

BUTTERCREAM SWIRL

The simplest buttercream finish is a swirl of icing. Put a spoonful of icing on the top of the cake, then hold the cake in one hand and swirl the icing with a knife, smoothing round the edge.

PIPING BUTTERCREAM

When piping icing – whether buttercream or royal icing – the easiest way to fill the piping (pastry) bag is to put the bag, fitted with the nozzle, in a tall mug or glass and roll down the bag. Spoon in the icing and then roll up the bag again. We find that disposable icing bags are a real labour-saver if you are piping in a number of different colours, since one of the most fiddly bits of washing up is trying to get a piping bag clean and dry.

We use mostly a large star piping nozzle to pipe the topping on to a cupcake. Start from the outside and pipe round, working your way towards the middle. We find that this makes it easier to cover the edges of the cake neatly (if that's what you want to do).

There is another sort of large nozzle that looks like a star nozzle but the metal tips are slightly more curved in. This produces an amazingly easy rose effect. Start piping from the centre with this one, working towards the outside, and it looks like a rose made of ribbons.

... *beat until thick and very white and forming pointy peaks.*

ROYAL ICING

We often use royal icing for topping cupcakes because it produces a thicker, more opaque and less fragile topping than glacé icing. Making it from scratch involves using raw egg white. If you are concerned about this, then you can use pasteurized egg white powder or pasteurized carton egg white instead. Alternatively, royal icing sugar – ready-mixed with pasteurized egg white powder – is now available and very convenient, especially for small quantities. We have given full instructions for royal icing wherever used, but if you have the ready-mixed sugar, then just use a little more than the amount of sugar specified in the recipe and follow the instructions on the packet. Whichever you use be sure to beat the icing thoroughly – at least 5 minutes with an electric whisk – otherwise it will not set properly.

The basic recipe produces icing that is thick enough for piping. Where royal icing is used as a base for further decoration, it is thinned with a little water until it just flows smoothly. One way of checking whether you have the right texture is to draw a knife through the icing and then count how long the mark takes to fill in. We find that a steady count of 15 will produce icing that flows smoothly but doesn't run all over the place.

If you are topping with sprinkles, you need to be ready to add them as soon as you have spread the icing. The surface dries quite quickly and once it is dry the sprinkles won't stick and just frustratingly bounce about.

115g/4oz/1 cup icing (confectioners') sugar
½ egg white (about 17g/½oz/generous 1 tbsp)
2.5ml/½ tsp glycerine

2.5ml/1 tsp lemon juice (optional)
5–7.5ml/1–1½ tsp water

▶▶ Makes enough for a smooth coating for 12 cupcakes

1 Sift the icing (confectioners') sugar and set aside. Beat the egg white until frothy and then gradually add the sugar, beating until the mixture is thick and glossy. Add the glycerine and lemon juice (if used) and continue beating until the mixture is thick and very white and forms pointy peaks when you lift the whisk. This will take at least 5 minutes with an electric whisk. If you do not need to use the icing immediately cover it closely with clear film (plastic wrap). At this point the icing is suitable for piping.

2 For coating icing, stir 1 tsp water into the icing and test the texture by drawing a knife through the icing and then counting how long the mark takes to fill in. Add a little more water if necessary until you reach the point where the mark fills in after a steady count of 15.

ITALIAN MERINGUE ICING

A shiny, fluffy, meringue-like topping is made by beating egg whites with sugar syrup. This is a whiter icing than buttercream and is good for pastel colours. It is great for a dramatic, glossy swirl of icing. The egg whites are partially cooked in the process, but if you prefer this icing can be made using reconstituted pasteurized dried egg white powder. It is best eaten on the day you make it – it hardens up if you keep it longer.

115g/4oz/generous ½ cup caster (superfine) sugar
90ml/3fl oz/6 tbsp water
2 egg whites
food colouring (optional)

▶▶ Makes enough to pipe swirls on 12 cupcakes

1 Place the sugar and water in a small heavy-based pan and heat gently until the sugar has completely dissolved. Wipe away any sugar crystals on the side of the pan with a pastry brush dipped in water. Increase the heat and boil without stirring until the temperature of the mixture reaches 119°C/238°F or a small amount of syrup dropped into a glass of cold water forms a soft ball.

2 Beat the egg whites with an electric whisk until they stand in soft peaks. Pouring the syrup down the side of the bowl and beating all the time, whisk until the mixture is stiff and glossy. Beat in the food colouring, if used, then spoon the mixture into a piping bag with a large star nozzle. Pipe swirls on the top of the cupcakes.

HOW TO MAKE A PAPER PIPING (PASTRY) BAG

If you have a small amount of fine piping to do, it can be convenient to use a small hand-made piping (pastry) bag made out of baking parchment.

1 Cut a right-angle triangle of paper with the short sides about 25–30cm/10–12in long. This can easily be done by cutting a 38cm/15in square of paper into quarters.

2 Hold the paper over the back of your hand with the right angle pointing to your elbow and wrap the paper into a cone with all three points crossing over at the top.

3 Turn in the points at the top to hold the cone in place. A piece of adhesive tape can also help to secure the cone. You may find that you have naturally created an opening at the point that is the right size for piping. If not, snip off a little bit of the point.

DECORATING

None of the normal rules apply when decorating cupcakes, more is definitely more. Look out for the unusual decorations and keep in a box ready for baking occasions, but don't worry if you don't have any fancy sprinkles. You can make very pretty cakes with little sweets, and it is very easy to make your own flags, toppers and wrappers for a very special result.

EDIBLE DECORATIONS

Even regular supermarkets are now stocking a great variety of edible decorations, and the range available from specialist online cake decoration suppliers sometimes seems unlimited. A plain vanilla sponge cupcake cake, topped with basic buttercream or glacé icing, will look magical with a sprinkling of hundreds and thousands, coloured sugar strands, edible pearls or one of the other hundreds of different types of sprinkles.

Edible sugar hearts and stars are easy to find, but we have also seen fishes, leaves, trees, pumpkins and little flowers. You can find ready-made larger sugar flowers, swirls and rosettes and roses. It is worth looking on the shelves of sprinkles designed for serving with ice cream for other ideas.

Edible glitter or lustre dusted over the icing gives a magical touch and although these usually come in very small containers a little goes a long way. They come in many different colours, but if you keep some silver or gold in your cupboard they will work with any colour of icing.

Coloured sugar sprinkles are also very effective. You can easily make these yourself. Put about 50g/2oz/¼ cup sugar in a screw-top jar. Add 2–3 drops of liquid food colouring (if you have gel or paste food colouring mix it with a little water first). Put on the lid and shake the jar until all the sugar is coloured. Spread the sugar on a plate and leave to dry out.

Old-fashioned glacé (candied) cherries, whole or cut in half, look very pretty on simple white or chocolate icing toppings. Single colourful jelly sweets (candies) can also look very attractive as do chocolate buttons and candy coated chocolate buttons (Smarties or M&Ms) and pieces of chocolate flake. Large silver, gold or pastel-coloured dragées might appeal to an older child.

FOOD COLOURING

We generally use gel or paste food colouring for icings because they are very concentrated so you don't need very much and they don't interfere with the texture of the icing. They are both becoming more widely available in supermarkets with good baking sections and cookshops as well as from specialist cake decorating shops and online suppliers. Liquid food colouring is more widely available and can be used to colour glacé icing, buttercream or royal icing (add it before adding any milk or juice to the buttercream as it will soften the icing), but it is not suitable for colouring ready-to-roll fondant icing. Add paste colouring a little at a time using a cocktail stick (toothpick) until you have the correct colour. It is very intense and you will only need a drop to produce a pastel pink, for example. Add gel colouring drop by drop until you get a feel for the strength of colour. The professional gels are quite strong but the gels available in supermarkets, though stronger than liquid colours, are less intense and you may need quite a lot for a batch of cakes.

add a sparkler ...

FOOD PENS AND WRITING ICING

Felt-tipped pens filled with edible ink are good for drawing designs on ready-to-roll fondant icing. Small tubes of ready-coloured icing are useful for little bits of piping. But if you cannot find these, you can make up a little coloured glacé icing with icing (confectioners') sugar and water and pipe this instead using a piping (pastry) bag with a nozzle or a cone of baking parchment with the end snipped off.

OTHER DECORATIONS

Cake candles now come in many colours, sizes and shapes – HAPPY BIRTHDAY sets, dinosaurs or butterflies for example. We especially like long thin candles sometimes called tapers. For older children miniature sparklers are great fun – straight ones and heart- or star-shaped sparklers are widely available.

Paper 'toppers', 'picks' or flags are a quick way to finish off a cupcake, and they are available ready-made in hundreds of different designs. Online sites will make paper toppers for you from uploaded photographs or other designs. They can also make edible discs of rice paper printed from your images.

It is very easy to make personalized flags yourself if you have access to a computer and a printer. Choose and crop your image and print multiple pairs of images measuring about 2.5cm/1in x 1cm/½in (5cm/2in long in total). Cut out the paper strips, wrap them round a cocktail stick (toothpick) and glue together. For a birthday party try making flags with pictures of the birthday boy or girl.

Pretty cupcake 'wrappers' are curved laser-cut strips of paper that can be wrapped round the finished cupcake. There are hundreds of different designs available online, but they are also easy to make. Create a template from a piece of stiff paper or light card. You can then cut the wrappers from colourful wrapping paper or use plain paper so that your child can have fun colouring them or decorating them with stickers. For a party, the wrappers could be personalized for each guest. Large, circular paper doilies are excellent for producing instant lace effects and decorative edges and come in plenty of different colours as well as gold and silver.

Glacé icing will look magical with a sprinkling of hundreds and thousands or edible pearls.

CAKE POPS

There are two ways of making these little cakes on a lollipop stick – baked or shaped. For baked cake pops, it is possible to buy non-stick cake pop tins (pans) that come in two halves, top and bottom, and produce little round balls of cake. These cake balls are suitable for recipes where the base is a simple round ball of cake, and are lighter than the shaped variety.

For cake pops in any shape other than a round ball, you need to use the alternative method of mixing cake crumbs with melted chocolate or buttercream, shaping the mixture into balls or other shapes and chilling. The bonus is that no special equipment is needed although the cake is rather richer – a plus or a minus depending on your point of view. This method works well with slightly stale cake and is a good way of using up leftover cake. The cake pops in this book have been made using these basic recipes.

VANILLA CAKE

115g/4oz/½ cup butter
115g/4oz/generous ½ cup caster (superfine) sugar
5ml/1 tsp vanilla extract
2 eggs, lightly beaten

115g/4oz/1 cup self-raising (self-rising) flour, sifted
15–30ml/1–2 tbsp milk

▶▶ **Makes enough cake for 20–24 pops**

1 Preheat the oven to 180°C/350°F/Gas 4. Line the baking tins (pans) – we used a large loaf tin roughly 21 x 10 x 7cm/8½ x 4 x 3in. But you could use a 20cm/8in round cake tin or two 18cm/7in sandwich tins.

2 Cream the butter for a few minutes until soft and pale. Add the sugar and continue to beat until the mixture is pale and fluffy. Add the vanilla extract to the lightly beaten eggs and then gradually add to the butter and sugar mixture, beating well between each addition. Add a teaspoon of flour with the last two additions so that the mixture does not curdle. Fold in the sifted flour and then 15–30ml/1–2 tbsp of milk so that the mixture drops slowly off the spoon.

3 Put the mixture into the lined cake tin. Put in the oven and cook for 45–50 minutes until risen, lightly browned and bouncy to the touch. Sandwich tin cakes will take about 25–30 minutes to cook. Cool the cake on a wire rack.

CHOCOLATE CAKE

90g/3½oz/¾ cup self-raising (self-rising) flour, sifted
25g/1oz/¼ cup unsweetened cocoa powder
115g/4oz/½ cup butter
115g/4oz/generous ½ cup caster (superfine) sugar
5ml/1 tsp vanilla extract

2 eggs, lightly beaten
15–30ml/1–2 tbsp milk

▶▶ **Makes enough cake for 20–24 pops**

1 Preheat the oven to 180°C/350°F/Gas 4. Sift the flour with the cocoa powder. Prepare the baking tins (pans) as for vanilla cake (above).

2 Cream the butter for a few minutes until soft and pale. Add the sugar and continue to beat until the mixture is pale and fluffy. Add the vanilla extract to the lightly beaten eggs and then gradually add to the butter and sugar mixture, beating well between each addition. Add a teaspoon of flour with the last two additions so that the mixture does not curdle. Fold in the sifted flour and then 15–30ml/1–2 tbsp of milk so that the mixture drops slowly off the spoon. Put the mixture into the lined cake tin and bake as above.

DECORATING CAKE POPS

Cake pop sticks (which are basically re-branded lollipop sticks) come in different lengths and are made of either plastic or paper. The long sticks – usually about 15cm/6in – are very elegant but shorter sticks (10cm/4in) are easier for children to manage. We find that paper sticks work better for us because the mixture seems to stick better. If you haven't got the mix just right the ball can slide disappointingly down the stick, and this seems to happen more often with the plastic variety.

We use a set of scales to measure the amount of mixture for each ball of mixture. It sounds a little obsessive, but the evenly sized balls you make will produce a more satisfying and professional result.

The single most useful piece of equipment for making cake pops is a block of polystyrene (Styrofoam) or florists' foam to stand the pops in to dry. You can often find a piece of polystyrene in the packing in a piece of electrical equipment. Cover it with clear film (plastic wrap) if you want to protect it against drops of chocolate. Whatever you do, work out how you are going to stand your pops up before you start dipping them, otherwise you will find yourself walking around the kitchen holding a dripping cake pop while you try to find something to support it.

Once baked or formed, cake pops are dipped in melted chocolate or a ready-coloured covering – either chocolate or a chocolate-style specialist coating called 'candy melts'. The candy melts are available as bags of buttons from specialist cake decorating shops or online. Chocolate buttons in a limited number of colours can be found in some supermarkets. White chocolate can be coloured with drops of gel or paste food colouring – but if you want really good colours you will need to use ready-coloured covering. The specialist coverings are also easier to manage for more complex designs as it sets more quickly than chocolate.

Place the chocolate or other covering in bowl. Use a relatively narrow bowl so that the melted covering will be quite deep, but not so narrow that you can't get a spoon in to help the process along. Melt the coating in a microwave or place the bowl over a pan of gently simmering water.

To coat the cake pop, dip the stick in the melted coating first, push it into the pop and then chill for a few minutes, if necessary, to secure the stick in place. Dip the pop again in the melted coating and spoon the coating over the pop to make sure it is fully covered. Tap the pop on the side of the bowl or twirl it gently around so that excess icing drops off. Stand the pop in polystyrene. Don't worry if the coating drips down the stick, it is easy to scrape off after it has set. However, be ready with any decorations – sugar sprinkles, small flowers, glitter – and sprinkle or stick them on while the coating is still wet.

Be ready with any decorations ...

WHOOPIE PIES

Chocolate mounds of cake sandwiched with white, fluffy icing have
a long history in the United States, but whoopie pies were less well known elsewhere
until recently. Now they are made in lots of different flavours as well as chocolate,
and kids love them!

Traditional whoopie pies are very large – sometimes 10cm/4in or more across – but in these recipes we suggest that
you make smaller ones. Whoopie pies are also traditionally made with buttermilk – a form of deliberately soured
milk that reacts with bicarbonate of soda (baking soda) to make the cakes rise. But, as buttermilk can be difficult to
find in some places, our recipes use conventional self-raising (self-rising) flour instead. The original whoopie pies did
not have icing on top, and we have kept decoration fairly simple so that they are not difficult to hold.

BASIC WHOOPIE PIE

75g/3oz/6 tbsp butter
130g/4½oz/scant ¾ cup caster (superfine) sugar
5ml/1 tsp vanilla extract
1 egg, lightly beaten
200g/7oz/1¾ cups self-raising (self-rising) flour

2.5ml/½ tsp baking powder
120ml/4fl oz/½ cup milk

▶▶ **Makes 16 small whoopie pies**

1 Preheat the oven to 190°C/375°F/Gas 5. Line two large baking sheets with baking parchment.

2 Cream the butter for a few minutes until soft and pale. Add the sugar, and continue to beat until the mixture is
pale and fluffy. Add the vanilla extract to the lightly beaten egg, and then gradually add to the butter and sugar
mixture, beating well between each addition.

3 Sift the flour with the baking powder. Stir half the flour into the mixture, then half the milk. Stir in the remaining
flour and then the remaining milk until the mixture is well combined, but don't over-mix.

4 Using a teaspoon, spoon 16 rounds of mixture on to each baking sheet – 32 in total. Bake for 10–12 minutes
until risen, lightly coloured and bouncy to the touch. Leave to cool on the baking sheets for a couple of minutes,
then transfer to a wire rack to cool.

Variation – Chocolate Whoopie Pies: Reduce the flour to 175g/6oz/1½ cups and sift together with 25g/1oz/
¼ cup unsweetened cocoa powder.

FILLING WHOOPIE PIES

You can use a simple buttercream or a more complicated marshmallow-type filling, depending on the recipe
you choose to follow. Feel free to mix and match the recipes for pies and fillings, to create your own
personal favourites.

1 Match the cakes up for shape and size. Use a teaspoon to place a spoonful of filling on to the flat side of one
cake, then spread it with a metal spatula. For a more professional-looking finish, pipe the filling on to the cake
using a piping (pastry) bag fitted with a star-shaped nozzle.

2 Gently press the flat side of the other cake on to the filling to make a sandwich, being careful not to squash the
filling out of the edges. Repeat with the remaining cakes and filling.

BEASTS, BUGS and Blooms

Lions and monkeys ... or other favourite animals?

Pretty primroses ...

Triceratops, stegosaurus and pterodactyl …

We love
farm animals,
especially pigs,
cows and sheep.

Whoopie pies are like a sandwich cake for one.

Orange and chocolate chip cupcakes with buttercream decoration make the perfect base for marmalade kittens and chocolate Labrador puppies. We like cats as well as dogs, but it is easy to adapt the design to make just kittens or puppies if you prefer, and if you have a favourite pet then just choose the cupcake cases, the buttercream colours and the shape of the ears to match your four-legged friend.

PUPPIES AND KITTENS

Attach the ears and pipe the mouths ...

FOR THE CAKES

115g/4oz/½ cup butter
115g/4oz/generous ½ cup caster (superfine) sugar
2 eggs, lightly beaten
115g/4oz/1 cup self-raising (self-rising) flour, sifted
100g/3¾oz milk chocolate chips
finely grated rind of 1 orange
15–30ml/1–2 tbsp orange juice

➡ **MAKES 12 CUPCAKES**

FOR THE DECORATION

25g/1oz plain (semi-sweet) chocolate
115g/4oz/½ cup butter, softened
225g/8oz/2 cups icing (confectioners') sugar, sifted
gel or paste food colouring, orange, brown, green, pink
5–10ml/1–2 tsp orange juice
5–10ml/1–2 tsp milk (optional)
100g/3¾oz ready-to-roll fondant icing, white
writing icing, white and black

1 Preheat the oven to 180°C/350°F/Gas 4. Line a muffin tin (pan) with cupcake cases.

2 Cream the butter for a few minutes until soft and pale. Add the sugar, and continue to beat until the mixture is pale and fluffy. Gradually add the eggs, beating well between each addition. Add a teaspoonful of flour with the last two additions so that the mixture does not curdle. Fold in the sifted flour, the chocolate chips and the orange rind, then enough of the orange juice so that the mixture drops slowly off the spoon.

3 Divide the mixture between the cupcake cases. Bake for 20–25 minutes until risen, lightly browned and bouncy to the touch. Take the cakes out of the oven, leave in the tin for a few minutes, then transfer to a wire rack to cool completely.

4 For the decoration, melt the chocolate in a microwave or in a heatproof bowl set over a pan of gently simmering water. Set aside to cool. Cream the butter for a few minutes until soft and light. Gradually add the sifted icing sugar, beating well between each addition.

5 Divide the buttercream in two. Colour one half pale orange with food colouring. Add the orange juice, a little at a time, until the buttercream is just soft enough to pipe.

6 Stir the cooled melted chocolate into the second half of the buttercream. If necessary, add the milk, a little at a time, until it is soft enough to pipe.

7 Colour one third of the ready-to-roll fondant icing orange, making it a slightly different shade from the buttercream. Colour another third brown, making it a different shade from the chocolate buttercream. Colour half the remaining icing light green and the rest pink (*see* p.148).

8 To make the kittens, pipe the orange buttercream on six of the cupcakes with a star nozzle. Roll out the orange icing and cut out 12 ears and six noses. Pinch the base of the ears together. Roll out the green icing and cut out 12 eyes. Allow the shapes to dry for a few minutes, then assemble the kitten faces and pipe the mouths and slits on the green eyes with black writing icing and whiskers with white writing icing.

9 To make the puppies, spread the chocolate buttercream on the other six cupcakes. Roll out the brown icing and cut out 12 ears, 12 eyes and six noses. Fold over the ears. Roll out the pink icing and cut out six tongues. Allow the shapes to dry for a few minutes, then assemble the puppy faces and pipe the mouths and irises on the eyes with the black writing icing.

Energy 333kcal/1354kJ; Protein 3g; Carbohydrate 51g, of which sugars 43g; Fat 13g, of which saturates 8g; Cholesterol 65mg; Calcium 63mg; Fibre 0g; Sodium 27mg

Variations

Simple lemon cupcakes would also work well as a base for the dinosaurs. The buttercream could be coloured bright blue or yellow. Chocolate-covered raisins could be used as 'prehistoric rocks'.

... pipe eyes with white and black icing.

FOR THE CAKES

115g/4oz/½ cup butter
115g/4oz/generous ½ cup caster (superfine) sugar
2 eggs, lightly beaten
115g/4oz/1 cup self-raising (self-rising) flour, sifted
50g/2oz/scant ⅔ cup desiccated (dry unsweetened shredded) coconut
finely grated rind of 1 lime
15–30ml/1–2 tbsp lime juice

FOR THE DECORATION

175g/6oz/¾ cup butter
350g/12oz/3 cups icing (confectioners') sugar, sifted
10–15ml/2–3 tsp lime juice
gel or paste food colouring, green, yellow, red, orange
175g/6oz ready-to-roll fondant icing, white
writing icing, red, white and black or coloured food pens
small sweets (candies)

➤➤ MAKES 12 CUPCAKES

1 Preheat the oven to 180°C/350°F/Gas 4. Line a muffin tin (pan) with cupcake cases.

2 Cream the butter for a few minutes until soft and pale. Add the sugar, and continue to beat until the mixture is pale and fluffy.

3 Gradually add the eggs, beating well between each addition. Add a teaspoonful of flour with the last two additions so that the mixture does not curdle.

4 Fold in the remaining sifted flour, the coconut and the lime rind, then add the lime juice, a little at a time, until the mixture drops slowly off the spoon.

5 Divide the mixture between the cupcake cases. Bake for 20–25 minutes until risen, lightly browned and bouncy to the touch. Take the cakes out of the oven, leave for a couple of minutes and then remove and cool on a rack.

6 For the decoration, cream the butter for a few minutes until soft and pale. Gradually add the sifted icing sugar, beating well between each addition. Beat in the lime juice, a little at a time, until the icing is just soft enough to pipe.

7 Colour the buttercream bright green with food colouring (*see* p.148). Pipe a mound of buttercream on each cupcake with a large star piping nozzle.

8 Divide the ready-to-roll fondant icing into four. Colour one portion green, one portion yellow and one portion red. Divide the remaining portion into three and colour the pieces pale green, pink and orange for features. Reserve a small amount of each colour, and then model 12 3D dinosaurs. Roll out the reserved portions, and cut out a variety of small flowers 0.5–1cm/¼–½in with cutters.

9 Perch one dinosaur on the top of each cupcake and place flowers and sweets in contrasting colours randomly around. Pipe white icing eyes and black pupils on each dinosaur with writing icing.

Nobody knows what colour prehistoric dinosaurs really were. Perhaps they were as brightly coloured as these cheerful characters? Lime and coconut cupcakes with lime buttercream decoration make a suitably tropical-tasting base, and once you get going you'll find that the 3D dinos are very quick and easy to model. We have made triceratops, stegosaurus and pterodactyl, but you can experiment with others.

Energy 454kcal/1904kJ; Protein 3g; Carbohydrate 62g, of which sugars 54g; Fat 24g, of which saturates 15g; Cholesterol 91mg; Calcium 48mg; Fibre 1g; Sodium 205mg

FARMYARD
FACES

FOR THE CAKES

115g/4oz/½ cup butter
115g/4oz/generous ½ cup caster (superfine) sugar
5ml/1 tsp vanilla extract
2 eggs, lightly beaten
115g/4oz/1 cup self-raising (self-rising) flour, sifted
15–30ml/1–2 tbsp milk

➡➡ MAKES 12 CUPCAKES

DECORATION

175g/6oz/1½ cups icing
  (confectioners') sugar
¾ egg white (about 25g/1oz/1½ tbsp)
5ml/1 tsp glycerine
5ml/1 tsp lemon juice (optional)
5–10ml/1–2 tsp water
175g/6oz ready-to-roll fondant icing
gel or paste food colouring, pink, brown, black
writing icing, black

Beat until the mixture is thick and very white.

We love farm animals, especially pigs, cows and sheep. Vanilla cupcakes have royal icing on top with features cut from ready-to-roll fondant icing. A set of little circle cookie cutters helps with cutting the shapes but it is usually possible to find circular things about the kitchen to use instead. You could try making horses, chicks, rabbits or ducklings as well.

1 Preheat the oven to 180°C/350°F/Gas 4. Line a muffin tin (pan) with cupcake cases.

2 Cream the butter for a few minutes until soft and pale. Add the sugar, and continue to beat until the mixture is pale and fluffy. Add the vanilla extract to the lightly beaten eggs and then gradually add to the butter and sugar mixture, beating well between each addition. Add a teaspoonful of flour with the last two additions so that the mixture does not curdle. Fold in the remaining sifted flour, and then add the milk, a little at a time, until the mixture drops slowly off the spoon.

3 Divide the mixture between the cupcake cases. Bake for 20–25 minutes until risen, lightly browned and bouncy to the touch. Take the cakes out of the oven, leave for a few minutes and then remove and cool on a rack.

4 For the decoration, sift the icing sugar and set aside. Beat the egg white until frothy and then gradually add the sugar, beating until the mixture is thick and glossy. Add the glycerine and lemon juice (if using) and continue beating until the mixture is thick and very white and forms pointy peaks when you lift the whisk. This will take at least 5 minutes with an electric whisk (*see* p.148).

5 Transfer about one-third of the icing to a piping (pastry) bag with a fine round nozzle, and pipe squiggly lines all over the top of four cupcakes to look like knitting. Keep any leftover icing in the bag for piping eyes later.

6 Stir 5ml/1 tsp water into the remaining icing in the bowl, and test the texture by drawing a knife through the icing and then counting how long the mark takes to fill in. Add a little more water if necessary until you reach the point where the mark fills in after a steady count of 15. Put half the icing in another bowl, and colour it pink with food colouring. Cover four cupcakes with white icing and four with pink.

7 Reserve about 25g/1oz of white ready-to-roll fondant icing (wrap it in clear film (plastic wrap) to stop it drying out). Colour one third of the remaining icing pink, one third brown and one third black.

8 For the pigs, roll out the pink ready-to-roll fondant icing to about 3–5mm/⅛–¼in thick and cut four round noses and eight pointy ears. Pinch the base of the ears gently together. For the cows, take the brown icing and cut four faces and eight ears (pinch the bases). Take the reserved white icing and cut four blotches and four noses. For the sheep, take the black icing and cut four faces and eight ears (pinch the bases). Arrange the pieces on the cupcakes.

9 Pipe eyes and noses on the sheep with the remaining white icing in the piping bag. Pipe eyes and nostrils on the cows and pigs with the black writing icing or colour a little royal icing black.

Energy 265kcal/117kJ; Protein 3g; Carbohydrate 46g, of which sugars 39g; Fat 9g, of which saturates 5g;
Cholesterol 60mg; Calcium 47mg; Fibre 0g; Sodium 118mg

Whoopie pies are like a sandwich cake for one.
The pies are traditionally much bigger, but we have made a smaller, more child-friendly version. We have decorated these whoopie pies with icing and flowers but they are also delicious without the topping.

Pipe buttercream on the flat side . . .

Cook's Tips
Pipe buttercream round the edge of the cake first and then pipe a star in the middle. When the two halves are put together any gaps in the icing will fill in.

SUMMER STRAWBERRY WHOOPIE PIES

FOR THE CAKES
75g/3oz/6 tbsp butter
130g/4½oz/scant ¾ cup caster (superfine) sugar
5ml/1 tsp vanilla extract
1 egg, lightly beaten
200g/7oz/1¾ cups self-raising (self-rising) flour
2.5ml/½ tsp baking powder
120ml/4fl oz/½ cup milk

➡ MAKES 16 SMALL WHOOPIE PIES

FOR THE FILLING
115g/4oz/½ cup butter, softened
225g/8oz/2 cups icing (confectioners') sugar, sifted
30ml/2 tbsp strawberry jam, sieved (strained)
5–10ml/1–2 tsp milk

FOR THE DECORATION
150g/5oz ready-to-roll fondant icing
gel or paste food colouring, yellow, green, red, pink
150g/5oz/1¼ cups icing (confectioners') sugar, sifted
30–40ml/2–2½ tbsp water or lemon juice

1 Preheat the oven to 190°C/375°F/Gas 5. Line two large baking sheets with baking parchment.

2 Cream the butter for a few minutes until soft and pale. Add the sugar, and continue to beat until the mixture is pale and fluffy. Add the vanilla extract to the lightly beaten egg, and then gradually add to the butter and sugar mixture, beating well between each addition. Sift the flour with the baking powder. Stir half the flour into the mixture, then half the milk. Stir in the remaining flour and then the remaining milk until the mixture is well combined, but don't over-mix.

3 Using a teaspoon, spoon 16 rounds of mixture on each baking sheet – 32 in total. Bake for 10–12 minutes until risen, lightly coloured and bouncy to the touch. Leave to cool on the baking sheets for a couple of minutes, then transfer to a wire rack to cool.

4 For the filling, cream the butter until soft and pale. Gradually add the sifted icing sugar, beating well between each addition. Beat in the sieved jam, and then add the milk (if necessary), a little at a time, until the icing is just soft enough to pipe.

5 Match up the cakes for size and shape. Pipe buttercream on the flat side of half the cakes using a large star piping nozzle (*see* p.148). Or, spread the buttercream using a knife or metal spatula. Sandwich the pairs together.

6 For the decoration, colour two-thirds of the ready-to-roll fondant icing yellow with food colouring. Colour the remaining icing green. Roll out and make large and small yellow five-petalled flowers. Colour red centres with food colouring. Make at least 32 little green leaves. Set aside to dry.

7 Mix the icing sugar with water or lemon juice, 5ml/1 tsp at a time, until just thin enough to spread. Be cautious as the icing starts to reach the right consistency. Colour the icing very pale pink.

8 Spread the pale pink icing on the filled pies and top each with flowers and leaves.

Energy 302kcal/1273kJ; Protein 2g; Carbohydrate 53g, of which sugars 44g; Fat 10g, of which saturates 6g; Cholesterol 41mg; Calcium 61mg; Fibre 1g; Sodium 147mg

WILD ANIMAL CAKE POPS

We have chosen lions and monkeys for these wildly chocolatey cake pops, but why not experiment with other favourite animals? We find that ready-coloured cake covering (chocolate buttons or candy melts available from specialist cake decorating shops or online stores) gives the strongest colouring and is easiest to work with so we have used them here, but you can use white chocolate coloured with gel or paste food colouring if you prefer.

FOR THE CAKE POPS
25g/1oz plain (semisweet) chocolate
65g/2½oz/5 tbsp butter, softened
150g/5oz/1¼ cups icing (confectioners') sugar, sifted
5–10ml/1–2 tsp milk (if required)
375g–400g/13–14oz chocolate cake
  (*see* recipe p.16 or use store-bought)

➤➤ **MAKES 20–24 CAKE POPS**

FOR THE DECORATION
175g/6oz ready-to-roll fondant icing, white
115g/4oz ready-to-roll fondant icing, black
gel or paste food colouring, brown
300g/11oz orange candy melts or coloured chocolate buttons
24 cake pop sticks
sugar strands and chocolate sprinkles
writing icing, black
vegetable oil (optional)

1 Melt the chocolate in a microwave or in a bowl over a pan of gently simmering water. Set aside to cool. Cream the butter until soft and pale. Gradually add the sifted icing sugar, beating well between each addition. Beat in the cooled, melted chocolate. If the icing is very stiff, add a little or all of the milk.

2 Crumble the cake into fine crumbs (this is easiest to do in a food processor) and place the crumbs in a large bowl. Mix in the buttercream, a spoonful at a time. The mixture needs to bind together and be mouldable, but not too wet. You may not need all of the buttercream, if your cake is very moist.

3 Shape the mixture into balls weighing about 25g/1oz each (*see* p.148). Shape half into long faces with cheeks for the lions and make the rest round. Chill the balls for at least 30 minutes until firm but not completely solid.

4 Take about a third of the white ready-to-roll fondant icing and make eyeballs 5–10mm/¼–½in across for the lions. Make smaller balls of black icing and press into the white balls for irises. Lions have quite pointy eyes rather than round ones. Make a set of black eyes 5–10mm/¼–½in across for the monkeys. Roll out the remaining black icing and cut out triangular noses for the lions. Colour the remaining white icing pale brown with the food colouring and roll out and cut faces for the monkeys. Press a pair of eyes on each. Make monkey ears from brown icing.

5 For the lions, melt the orange covering in a microwave or in a heatproof bowl set over a pan of gently simmering water. Dip a stick in the covering and then insert it about halfway into a ball. Repeat with the remaining balls and, if necessary, chill until firm. Dip a whole lion cake pop in the covering, using a spoon if necessary to help with covering the cake. If the covering is too thick, thin with a little vegetable oil (not water). Gently tap and twirl to shake off excess.

6 Press on black eyes, nose and muzzle details, and cover the back of the lion's head with sugar strands. Stick the pop into a block of polystyrene (Styrofoam) or florists' foam and leave to dry or chill. Repeat with the rest of the lion pops.

7 Now make the monkeys. If necessary re-warm the remaining covering. Add brown gel or paste food colouring to turn the covering brown. Dip a whole monkey cake pop into the covering. Gently tap and twirl to shake off excess. Press on the ears and face and cover the whole head with chocolate sprinkles. Stick the pop into a block of polystyrene or florists' foam and leave to dry or chill. Repeat with the rest of the monkey pops. When the pops have set, draw on mouths and nostrils with writing icing.

Energy 235kcal/986kJ; Protein 2g; Carbohydrate 33g, of which sugars 30g;
Fat 11g, of which saturates 7g; Cholesterol 39mg; Calcium 50mg; Fibre 0g; Sodium 92mg

It must be the red jackets and cheerful spots that make ladybirds (ladybugs) so popular – unlike most other insects. We have used chocolate buttons for the spots on these whoopies filled with chocolate buttercream, but candy-coated chocolates or chocolate chips would work as well.

LUCKY BUG WHOOPIE PIES

FOR THE CAKES
75g/3oz/6 tbsp butter
130g/4½oz/¾ cup soft light brown sugar
5ml/1 tsp vanilla extract
1 egg, lightly beaten
175g/6oz/1½ cups self-raising (self-rising) flour
2.5ml/½ tsp baking powder
25g/1oz/¼ cup unsweetened cocoa powder
120ml/4fl oz/½ cup milk

▶▶ MAKES 16 SMALL WHOOPIE PIES

FOR THE FILLING
50g/2oz plain (semisweet) chocolate
115g/4oz/½ cup butter, softened
225g/8oz/2 cups icing (confectioners') sugar, sifted
5–10ml/1–2 tsp milk (optional)

FOR THE DECORATION
50g/2oz ready-to-roll fondant icing, black
25g/1oz ready-to-roll fondant icing, white
175g/6oz/1½ cups icing (confectioners') sugar, sifted
30–40ml/2–2½ tbsp water
gel or paste food colouring, red
32–48 flat chocolate discs
writing icing, black

1 Preheat the oven to 190°C/375°F/Gas 5. Line two large baking sheets with baking parchment.

2 Cream the butter for a few minutes until soft and pale. Add the sugar, and continue to beat until the mixture is pale and fluffy. Add the vanilla extract to the lightly beaten egg and then gradually add to the butter and sugar mixture, beating well between each addition. Sift the flour with the baking powder and cocoa. Stir half the flour into the mixture, then stir in half the milk. Stir in the remaining flour and then the remaining milk until the mixture is well combined, but don't over mix.

3 Using a teaspoon, spoon 16 rounds of mixture on each baking sheet – 32 in total. Bake for 10–12 minutes until risen, lightly coloured and bouncy to the touch. Leave to cool on the baking sheets for a couple of minutes, then transfer to a wire rack to cool.

4 For the filling, melt the chocolate in a microwave or in a bowl over a pan of gently simmering water. Set aside to cool. Cream the butter until soft and pale. Gradually add the sifted icing sugar, beating well between each addition. Beat in the chocolate and then the milk, a little at a time, until the icing is just soft enough to pipe.

5 Match up the cakes for size and shape. Pipe buttercream on the flat side of half the cakes using a large star piping nozzle or spread the buttercream with a knife. Sandwich the pairs together.

6 To make the heads, roll out the black ready-to-roll fondant icing and cut 16 discs about 2.5–3cm/1–1¼in across. Roll out the white icing. Cut eyes and press into the black discs (*see* p.149). Set aside to dry.

7 Mix the icing sugar with water just 5ml/1 tsp at a time until just thin enough to spread, but still fairly stiff. Use a little white icing to pipe on mouths, then colour the rest red and spread on the top of each whoopie pie (*see* p.149). When the icing has stopped flowing, stick a head on each pie and two or four chocolate discs for spots (secure these with black icing, if you prefer). Use the black writing icing to make dots in the eyes.

Energy 210kcal/883kJ; Protein 2g; Carbohydrate 34g, of which sugars 28g; Fat 8g, of which saturates 5g; Cholesterol 28mg; Calcium 46mg; Fibre 0g; Sodium 106mg

FLUTTERBY BUTTERFLY CAKES

Butterfly cakes were a children's party treat long before cupcakes became fashionable. The method of scooping a disc out of the top of the cupcake and cutting it in two to form butterfly wings can be used with any sort of cupcake and some people use jam to hold the wings together but we like lemon buttercream. We have cut the extra wings out of ready-to-roll fondant icing, but you can also easily find pretty wafer or ready-made sugarpaste butterflies.

FOR THE CAKES

115g/4oz/½ cup butter
115g/4oz/generous ½ cup caster (superfine) sugar
2 eggs, lightly beaten
115g/4oz/1 cup self-raising (self-rising) flour, sifted
finely grated rind of 1 lemon
15–30ml/1–2 tbsp lemon juice

▶ MAKES 12 CUPCAKES

FOR THE DECORATION

a sheet of light card
75g/3oz ready-to-roll fondant icing, white
gel or paste food colouring, pink and blue
edible pearls
50g/2oz/¼ cup butter
115g/4oz/1 cup icing (confectioners') sugar, sifted
5ml/1 tsp lemon juice

1 Preheat the oven to 180°C/350°F/Gas 4. Line a muffin tin (pan) with cupcake cases.

2 Cream the butter for a few minutes until soft and pale. Add the sugar, and continue to beat until the mixture is pale and fluffy. Gradually add the eggs, beating well between each addition. Add a teaspoonful of flour with the last two additions so that the mixture does not curdle. Fold in the sifted flour and the lemon rind, then add the lemon juice, a little at a time, until the mixture drops slowly off the spoon.

3 Divide the mixture between the cupcake cases. Bake for 20–25 minutes until risen, lightly browned and bouncy to the touch. Allow to cool in the tin for a couple of minutes, then transfer to a wire rack to cool completely.

4 For the decoration, fold the sheet of card lengthways into four to form a gutter and grease lightly. Colour half the ready-to-roll fondant icing pale pink and the other half pale blue. Roll out and cut butterfly shapes about 4.5cm/1¾in across. Crease lightly along the centre and place in the folded paper gutter. Press edible pearls into each wing and leave to dry (see p.149).

5 Cream the butter for a few minutes until soft and pale. Gradually add the sifted icing sugar, beating well between each addition. Beat in 5ml/1tsp of lemon juice.

6 Cut a shallow, circular scoop out of the top of each cake. Put a teaspoonful of buttercream into each scoop. Cut the pieces of cake in two and place on the top of the buttercream to form wings. Position an icing butterfly on top of each cake.

Energy 246kcal/1030kJ; Protein 2g; Carbohydrate 33g, of which sugars 26g; Fat 13g, of which saturates 7g; Cholesterol 69mg; Calcium 44mg; Fibre 0g; Sodium 136mg

Pretty primroses top moist carrot cupcakes and delicious cream cheese frosting.
We have made the flowers with ready-to-roll fondant icing and found some clever cutters that make
a primrose petal shape, but it is possible to shape very sweet flowers without cutters. Cutters for
rose leaves produce leaves that look quite like primrose leaves, especially if you stretch them a little.
If you are short of time, it is easy to find ready-made edible flowers of all kinds, or top the cakes
with sugared fresh flowers if your child likes the idea.

SPRINGTIME FLOWERS

Cover each cupcake with a shallow swirl of icing …

FOR THE CAKES

115g/4oz/1 cup self-raising (self-rising) flour
2.5ml/½ tsp ground cinnamon
1.5ml/¼ tsp ground ginger
pinch of salt
115g/4oz/generous ½ cup soft brown sugar
120ml/4fl oz/½ cup sunflower oil
2 eggs, lightly beaten
115g/4oz grated carrot
  (approximately 175g/6oz whole carrots)
finely grated rind of 1 orange
50g/2oz/⅓ cup raisins (optional)

FOR THE DECORATION

40g/1½oz/3 tbsp butter, softened
115g/4oz/½ cup cream cheese, cold
250g/9oz/2¼ cups icing (confectioners') sugar, sifted
150g/5oz ready-to-roll fondant icing, white
gel or paste food colouring: yellow, pink, green

➠ **MAKES 12 CUPCAKES**

1 Preheat the oven to 180°C/350°F/Gas 4. Line a muffin tin (pan) with cupcake cases. Sift the flour with the cinnamon, ginger and salt and set aside.

2 Put the sugar, oil and eggs in a large bowl and beat together until smooth. Add the grated carrot to the mixture with the flour and spices, orange rind and raisins if used.

3 Divide the mixture between the cupcake cases. Bake for 20–25 minutes until risen, lightly browned and bouncy to the touch. Take the cakes out of the oven, leave in the tin for a few minutes, then transfer to a wire rack to cool completely.

4 For the decoration, cream the butter for a few minutes until soft and pale. Drain the cream cheese and beat together with the butter until combined (*see* p.149). Don't overbeat. Add half the sifted icing sugar and beat until combined, then beat in the remaining sugar. Chill until ready to use.

5 Divide the ready-to-roll fondant icing into three portions. Colour one portion pale yellow and one portion pale pink. You will only need a very small amount of colour to produce the pale shades. Colour the remaining icing leaf green. Cut out and shape primrose petals from the yellow and pale pink icing. Colour the centres with a little yellow food colouring on a cocktail stick (toothpick). Cut leaves from the green icing. Set aside until dry.

6 Cover each cupcake with a shallow swirl of cream cheese icing then decorate with the flowers and leaves.

Energy 361kcal/1515kJ; Protein 2g; Carbohydrate 33g, of which sugars 46g; Fat 18g, of which saturates 6g; Cholesterol 20mg; Calcium 53mg; Fibre 1g; Sodium 96mg

FESTIVE
Treats

*Sometimes only a cupcake
will do for a celebration.*

Bright colours and flags are just right for a birthday.

Fix two black eyes, a carrot nose and three buttons.

HAPPY BIRTHDAY
CUPCAKES

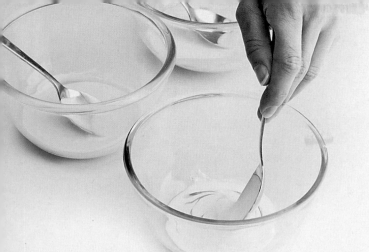

Decorate with sprinkles before the icing sets.

FOR THE CAKES

115g/4oz/½ cup butter
115g/4oz/generous ½ cup caster (superfine) sugar
5ml/1 tsp vanilla extract
2 eggs, lightly beaten
115g/4oz/1 cup self-raising (self-rising) flour, sifted
15–30ml/1–2 tbsp milk

➡ MAKES 12 CUPCAKES

FOR THE DECORATION

115g/4oz/1 cup icing (confectioners') sugar
½ egg white (about 17g/½oz/generous 1 tbsp)
2.5ml/½ tsp glycerine
2.5ml/½ tsp lemon juice (optional)
5–7.5ml/1–1½ tsp water
gel or paste food colouring, green, blue, yellow
brightly coloured sugar sprinkles
candles

1 Preheat the oven to 180°C/350°F/Gas 4. Line a muffin tin (pan) with cupcake cases.

2 Cream the butter for a few minutes until soft and pale. Add the sugar, and continue to beat until the mixture is pale and fluffy. Add the vanilla extract to the lightly beaten eggs, and then gradually add to the butter and sugar mixture, beating well between each addition. Add a teaspoonful of flour with the last two additions, so that the mixture does not curdle. Fold in the sifted flour, and then stir in the milk, a little at a time, until the mixture drops slowly off the spoon.

3 Divide the mixture between the cupcake cases. Bake for 20–25 minutes until risen, lightly browned and bouncy to the touch. Allow the cakes to cool in the tin for a few minutes, then transfer to a wire rack to cool completely.

4 For the decoration, sift the icing sugar and set aside. Beat the egg white until frothy, and then gradually add the sugar, beating until the mixture is thick and glossy. Add the glycerine and lemon juice (if using) and continue beating until the mixture is thick, very white and forms pointy peaks when you lift the whisk. This will take at least 5 minutes with an electric whisk.

5 Stir 5ml/1 tsp water into the icing and test the texture by drawing a knife through the icing and then counting how long the mark takes to fill in (*see* p.149). Add a little more water, if necessary, until you reach the point where the mark fills in after a steady count of 15.

6 Divide the icing into three bowls, and colour each portion with the food colouring. Cover four cupcakes with each of the icing colours and then decorate with sprinkles before the icing sets.

7 Arrange the cupcakes on a cake stand or board and decorate with candles.

Bright colours, candles and flags are just the thing for a birthday. We particularly like spotted candles, but you can find them in a huge variety of shapes from numbers and letters to dinosaurs and butterflies. Top as many cakes as the child's age with candles. You can use flags or make your own cake toppers with pairs of a favourite picture printed out and glued round a cocktail stick (toothpick) for the remaining cakes.

Energy 194kcal/814kJ; Protein 2g; Carbohydrate 27g, of which sugars 20g; Fat 9g, of which saturates 5g; Cholesterol 60mg; Calcium 44mg; Fibre 0g; Sodium 109mg

FOR THE CAKES

115g/4oz/1 cup self-raising (self-rising) flour
2.5ml/½ tsp ground cinnamon
115g/4oz/½ cup butter, softened
115g/4oz/generous ½ cup caster (superfine) sugar
2 eggs, lightly beaten
grated rind of 1 orange
15–30ml/1–2 tbsp orange juice

FOR THE DECORATION

115g/4oz/1 cup icing (confectioners') sugar
½ egg white (about 17g/½oz/generous 1 tbsp)
2.5ml/½ tsp glycerine
2.5ml/½ tsp lemon juice (optional)
5–7.5ml/1–1½ tsp water
200g/7oz ready-to-roll fondant icing, white
gel or paste food colouring, red and bright green
edible silver pearls and stars
edible glitter

Cook's Tips

We used a daisy-shaped cutter for the wreath discs, but they will look just as good with leaves cut out with a plain round cutter.

➡➡ MAKES 12 CUPCAKES

CHRISTMAS CUPCAKES

Orange and cinnamon give a Christmassy flavour to these glittery red, white and green cupcakes. Look out for little cookie cutters in festive shapes; they are great for cutting shapes from ready-to-roll fondant icing. Bold simple shapes work best.

1 Preheat the oven to 180°C/350°F/Gas 4. Line a muffin tin (pan) with cupcake cases. Sift the flour with the cinnamon and set aside.

2 Cream the butter for a few minutes until soft and pale. Add the sugar, and continue to beat until the mixture is pale and fluffy. Gradually add the lightly beaten eggs to the butter and sugar mixture, beating well between each addition. Add a teaspoonful of flour with each of the last two additions, so that the mixture does not curdle. Fold in the sifted flour and the grated rind, then add the orange juice, a little at a time, until the mixture drops slowly off the spoon.

3 Divide the mixture between the cupcake cases. Bake for 20–25 minutes until risen, lightly browned and bouncy to the touch. Take the cakes out of the oven, allow to cool in the tin for a couple of minutes, then transfer to a wire rack to cool completely.

4 For the decoration, sift the icing sugar and set aside. Beat the egg white until frothy (*see* p.149) and then gradually add the sugar, beating until the mixture is thick and glossy. Add the glycerine and lemon juice (if used) and continue beating until the mixture is thick and very white and forms pointy peaks when you lift the whisk. This will take at least 5 minutes with an electric whisk.

5 Stir 5ml/1 tsp water into the icing and test the texture by drawing a knife through the icing and then counting how long the mark takes to fill in. Add a little more water, if necessary, until you reach the point where the mark fills in after a steady count of 15. Cover the cupcakes with icing.

6 Colour half the ready-to-roll fondant icing red and the other green with the food colouring. Cut four green Christmas trees. Arrange on cakes and decorate with edible silver pearls and a star. Cut out four red snowflakes and decorate with a star. For the wreaths cut 20 green discs about 2cm/¾in across and 20 red discs. Arrange nine green discs and one red disc in a circle on top of two of the remaining cupcakes and the reverse on the last two. Dust the cakes lightly with edible glitter.

Energy 251kcal/1058kJ; Protein 2g; Carbohydrate 43g, of which sugars 35g; Fat 9g, of which saturates 5g; Cholesterol 60mg; Calcium 44mg; Fibre 0g; Sodium 113mg

CHRISTMAS TREE CUPCAKES

Cook's Tips

Tweezers will help with positioning the sugar pearls on the trees which can be fiddly.

A forest of little green buttercream Christmas trees tops these white chocolate chip cupcakes. If you prefer a snow-covered forest, leave the buttercream uncoloured. We have used sugar pearls to decorate the trees but you could try any miniature sugar shapes.

FOR THE CAKES

115g/4oz/½ cup butter
115g/4oz/generous ½ cup caster (superfine) sugar
2.5ml/½ tsp vanilla extract
2 eggs, lightly beaten
115g/4oz/1 cup self-raising (self-rising) flour, sifted
75g/3oz white chocolate chips
15–30ml/1–2 tbsp milk

➡ MAKES 12 CUPCAKES

FOR THE DECORATION

115g/4oz/½ cup butter, softened
225g/8oz/2 cups icing (confectioners') sugar, sifted
5ml/1 tsp vanilla extract
5–10ml/1–2 tsp milk
gel or paste food colouring, green
edible sugar pearls
12 edible stars
edible glitter

1 Preheat the oven to 180°C/350°F/Gas 4. Line a muffin tin (pan) with cupcake cases.

2 Cream the butter for a few minutes until soft and pale. Add the sugar, and continue to beat until the mixture is pale and fluffy. Add the vanilla extract to the lightly beaten eggs, and then gradually add to the butter and sugar mixture, beating well between each addition. Add a teaspoonful of flour with the last two additions so that the mixture does not curdle.

3 Fold in the sifted flour and the chocolate chips, then stir in the milk, a little at a time, until the mixture drops slowly off the spoon.

4 Divide the mixture between the cupcake cases. Bake for 20–25 minutes until risen, lightly browned and bouncy to the touch. Allow the cakes to cool in the tin for a few minutes, then transfer to a wire rack to cool completely.

5 For the decoration, cream the butter for a few minutes until soft and light. Gradually add the sifted icing sugar, beating well between each addition. Beat in the vanilla extract, and then add the milk, a little at a time, until the icing is just soft enough to pipe.

6 Spread a thin layer of buttercream over all of the cupcakes (*see* p.150). Colour the remaining buttercream green, using the food colouring gel or paste.

7 Using a piping (pastry) bag with a star-shaped nozzle, pipe green buttercream Christmas trees on each cupcake. Decorate with small sugar pearls and top each tree with a star. Dust the cupcakes with edible glitter.

Energy 334kcal/1399kJ; Protein 3g; Carbohydrate 41g, of which sugars 33g; Fat 19g, of which saturates 11g; Cholesterol 81mg; Calcium 63mg; Fibre 0g; Sodium 175mg

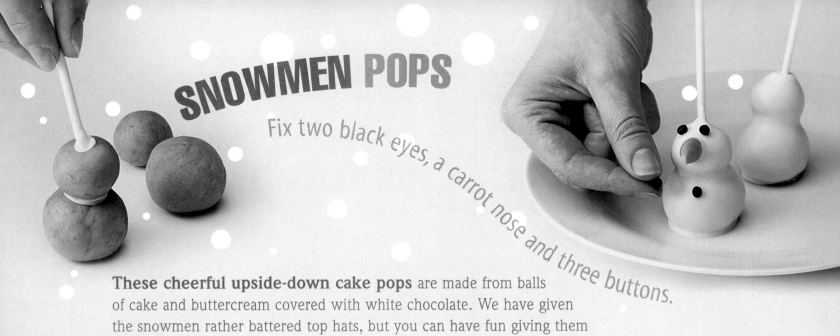

SNOWMEN POPS

Fix two black eyes, a carrot nose and three buttons.

These cheerful upside-down cake pops are made from balls of cake and buttercream covered with white chocolate. We have given the snowmen rather battered top hats, but you can have fun giving them individual hats and scarves.

FOR THE CAKE POPS
65g/2½oz/5 tbsp butter, softened
150g/5oz/1¼ cups icing (confectioners') sugar, sifted
5–10ml/1–2 tsp milk
375–400g/13–14oz vanilla or lemon cake
  (*see* recipe p.16 or use store-bought)

➤➤ **MAKES 15–16 CAKE POPS**

FOR THE DECORATION
100g/3¾oz ready-to-roll fondant icing, black
100g/3¾oz ready-to-roll fondant icing, white
300g/11oz white candy melts or white chocolate
gel or paste food colouring, orange, red, blue
cake pop sticks
5ml/1 tsp icing (confectioners') sugar, for dusting

1 Cream the butter until soft and pale. Gradually add the sifted icing sugar, beating well between each addition. If the icing is very stiff, add a little or all of the milk.

2 Crumble the cake into fine crumbs (this is easiest to do in a food processor) and place the crumbs in a large bowl. Mix in the buttercream, a spoonful at a time (*see* p.150). The mixture needs to bind together and be mouldable but not too wet. You may not need all the buttercream, if your cake is very moist.

3 Shape the mixture into 15–16 round balls weighing about 25g/1oz for the bodies and 15–16 round balls weighing about 10g/¼oz for the heads. Chill the balls for about 30 minutes, until firm but not completely solid.

4 For the decoration, take about a quarter of the black ready-to-roll fondant icing and make at least 75 tiny balls 3mm/⅛in across for the snowman's eyes and buttons. Take a quarter of the white icing, colour it orange and make carrot noses about 1cm/½in long. Set aside to dry.

5 Melt the white candy melts or white chocolate carefully in a microwave or in a heatproof bowl set over a pan of gently simmering water. Dip the base of one head into the white covering, and stick to the top of a body. Then dip a pop stick in the melted white covering, and insert it through the head and halfway through the body. Repeat with the remaining balls of cake, and then chill until firm.

6 Lightly oil a plate. Reheat the white melts or chocolate, until melted again. Holding the stick, dip a whole snowman in melted white covering to coat completely. Tap and twirl to remove excess chocolate, and then stand on the plate. Fix two black eyes, a carrot nose and three buttons on each snowman. Chill until firm.

7 Take the remaining black icing, mould top hats and press them round the sticks of each snowman. Colour the remaining white icing red and blue. Roll out and cut strips about 13cm/5in for scarves. Wrap the scarves round the snowmen's necks. Dust with icing sugar.

Energy 326kcal/1369kJ; Protein 3g; Carbohydrate 44g, of which sugars 40g; Fat 16g, of which saturates 10g;
Cholesterol 54mg; Calcium 86mg; Fibre 0g; Sodium 131mg

CHINESE DRAGON

Almond and lemon cupcakes provide an appropriately Chinese flavour for this rather friendly dragon. Bake the cakes in shiny red or gold cupcake cases to add to the Chinese effect. Ten of the cakes form the body of the dragon with colourful scales, one cake has the dragon's head and the other his tail. You can easily make the dragon bigger by extending the dragon's body with more cupcakes.

FOR THE CAKES

75g/3oz/⅔ cup self-raising (self-rising) flour
5ml/1 tsp baking powder
115g/4oz/½ cup butter, softened
115g/4oz/generous ½ cup caster (superfine) sugar
1.5ml/¼ tsp almond extract
2 eggs, lightly beaten
50g/2oz/½ cup ground almonds
finely grated rind of 1 lemon
15–30ml/1–2 tbsp lemon juice

➡➡ **MAKES 12 CUPCAKES**

DECORATION

450g/1lb ready-to-roll fondant icing, white
gel or paste food colouring, yellow, red
writing icing, black, red
115g/4oz/½ cup butter, softened
225g/8oz/2 cups icing (confectioners') sugar, sifted
5–10ml/1–2 tsp lemon juice
gold and red edible glitter

1 Preheat the oven to 180°C/350°F/Gas 4. Line a muffin tin (pan) with cupcake cases. Sift the flour with the baking powder and set aside.

2 Cream the butter for a few minutes until soft and pale. Add the sugar, and continue to beat until the mixture is pale and fluffy. Add the almond extract to the lightly beaten eggs, and then gradually add to the butter and sugar mixture, beating well between each addition. Add a teaspoonful of flour with each of the last two additions so that the mixture does not curdle. Fold in the sifted flour, almonds and the grated rind, then add the lemon juice, a little at a time, until the mixture drops slowly off the spoon.

3 Divide the mixture between the cupcake cases. Bake for 20–25 minutes until risen, lightly browned and bouncy to the touch. Allow to cool in the tin for a couple of minutes, then transfer to a wire rack to cool completely.

4 Reserve about 50g/2oz of the white ready-to-roll fondant icing and wrap tightly in clear film (plastic wrap). Divide the remaining icing in half, and colour one portion yellow and the other portion red.

5 Form the tail and head (roughly the shape of a small brick with rounded corners) with the red icing. Cut a mouth in the head and insert a piece of white icing (*see* p.150). Mark teeth with a sharp knife. Form eyes with the white icing, stick to the head and mark pupils with the black writing icing. Roll-out the yellow icing and cut out ten scales for the body cupcakes and additional scales to adorn the head and the tail. Set aside to dry.

6 Cream the butter until soft and pale. Gradually add the icing sugar, beating between each addition. Beat in the lemon juice, a little at a time, until the icing is just soft enough to pipe. Colour the icing red with food colouring. Pipe icing on each of the cupcakes using a star piping nozzle.

7 Position the scales on ten of the cupcakes, then position the head and tail on the remaining cupcakes. Draw lines on the scales with red writing icing. Dust the cupcakes with edible glitter. Arrange the cakes in a curving line with head and tail at the ends.

Energy 444kcal/1869kJ; Protein 3g; Carbohydrate 69g, of which sugars 64g; Fat 19g, of which saturates 10g; Cholesterol 81mg; Calcium 50mg; Fibre 1g; Sodium 206mg

Cook's Tips

If you warm the spoon first in hot water, it will make it easier to measure the syrup.

CHOCOLATE NEST CUPCAKES

... gently stir in the cornflakes.

Two favourite Easter treats come together in these chocolate cupcakes topped with crunchy chocolate nests and mini chocolate eggs. This recipe is made with plain (semisweet) chocolate, but if your children prefer you could do half and half with milk chocolate. We used deeper muffin cases rather than regular cupcake cases to support the nests on top of the cakes.

FOR THE CAKES
90g/3½oz/¾ cup self-raising (self-rising) flour
25g/1oz/¼ cup unsweetened cocoa powder
115g/4oz/½ cup butter
115g/4oz/scant ¾ cup soft light brown sugar
2 eggs, lightly beaten
15–30ml/1–2 tbsp milk

FOR THE NESTS
100g/3½oz plain (semisweet) chocolate
15ml/1 tbsp golden (light corn) syrup
25g/1oz/2 tbsp butter
75g/3oz cornflakes or crisped rice cereal
36 mini chocolate eggs (approximately 150g/5oz)

➡ MAKES 12 CUPCAKES

1 Preheat the oven to 180°C/350°F/Gas 4. Line a muffin tin (pan) with cupcake cases.

2 Sift together the flour and the cocoa powder (*see* p.150), and set aside.

3 Cream the butter for a few minutes until soft and pale. Add the sugar and continue to beat until the mixture is pale and fluffy.

4 Gradually add the lightly beaten eggs to the butter and sugar mixture, beating well between each addition. Add a teaspoonful of flour with each of the last two additions so that the mixture does not curdle.

5 Fold in the sifted flour and cocoa, and then add the milk, a little at a time, until the mixture drops slowly off the spoon.

6 Divide the mixture between the cupcake cases. Bake for 20–25 minutes until risen, lightly browned and bouncy to the touch. Allow to cool in the tin for a few minutes, and then remove and cool on a rack.

7 For the nests, melt the chocolate, golden syrup and butter in a microwave or in a heatproof bowl set over a pan of gently simmering water. Remove from the heat, and gently stir in the cornflakes or crisped rice cereal. Divide the mixture between the cupcakes and make a dip in the middle of each nest. Arrange three chocolate eggs in the middle of each nest, then chill until the nests have set.

Energy 279kcal/1168kJ; Protein 4g; Carbohydrate 29g, of which sugars 23g; Fat 17g, of which saturates 10g; Cholesterol 68mg; Calcium 75mg; Fibre 0g; Sodium 150mg

We have decorated these vanilla cupcakes in red, white and blue, but you could choose any combination of colours depending on the occasion. We made the flags ourselves by cutting out double-length strips of coloured paper and gluing them around cocktail sticks (toothpicks).

FLYING THE FLAG CUPCAKES

Variations

If you are short of time, glacé icing (*see* p.10) can be used instead of the royal icing.

FOR THE CAKES

115g/4oz/½ cup butter
115g/4oz/generous ½ cup caster (superfine) sugar
5ml/1 tsp vanilla extract
2 eggs, lightly beaten
115g/4oz/1 cup self-raising (self-rising) flour, sifted
15–30ml/1–2 tbsp milk

➤➤ MAKES 12 CUPCAKES

FOR THE DECORATION

115g/4oz/1 cup icing (confectioners') sugar
½ egg white (about 17g/½oz/generous 1 tbsp)
2.5ml/½ tsp glycerine
2.5ml/½ tsp lemon juice (optional)
5–7.5ml/1–1½ tsp water
red, white and blue sprinkles and small sweets (candies)
12 red, white and blue flags

1 Preheat the oven to 180°C/350°F/Gas 4. Line a muffin tin (pan) with cupcake cases.

2 Cream the butter for a few minutes until soft and pale. Add the sugar, and continue to beat until the mixture is pale and fluffy.

3 Add the vanilla extract to the lightly beaten eggs, and then gradually add to the butter and sugar mixture, beating well between each addition. Add a teaspoonful of flour with the last two additions so that the mixture does not curdle.

4 Fold in the sifted flour, and add the milk, a little at a time, until the mixture drops slowly off the spoon (*see* p.150).

5 Divide the mixture between the cupcake cases. Bake for 20–25 minutes until risen, lightly browned and bouncy to the touch. Allow to cool in the tin for a few minutes, then transfer to a wire rack, and allow to cool completely.

6 For the decoration, sift the icing sugar and set aside. Beat the egg white until frothy and then gradually add the sugar, beating until the mixture is thick and glossy. Add the glycerine and lemon juice (if using), and continue beating until the mixture is thick, very white and forms peaks when you lift the whisk. This will take at least 5 minutes with an electric whisk.

7 Stir 5ml/1 tsp water into the icing, then test the texture by drawing a knife through the icing and then counting how long the mark takes to fill in. Add a little more water, if necessary, until you reach the point where the mark fills in after a steady count of 15.

8 Ice the cupcakes with royal icing. Decorate with sprinkles and sweets and then stick a flag in each.

Energy 193kcal/813kJ; Protein 2g; Carbohydrate 27g, of which sugars 20g; Fat 9g, of which saturates 5g; Cholesterol 60mg; Calcium 42mg; Fibre 0g; Sodium 111mg

You can really go to town with the decoration ideas for these gruesome red velvet cupcakes. We've had fun with knives and eyeballs liberally sprinkled with raspberry jam blood, but you could also try bats or tombstones cut out of grey ready-to-roll fondant icing. The knives need about an hour to dry until they are strong enough to be placed on the cupcakes.

FRIGHT NIGHT CUPCAKES

Variations

If your child has an aversion to cheese, then you can use vanilla buttercream instead of the cream cheese icing.

FOR THE CAKES

90g/3½oz/¾ cup self-raising (self-rising) flour
10g/¼oz/1 tbsp unsweetened cocoa powder
115g/4oz/½ cup butter
115g/4oz/generous ½ cup caster (superfine) sugar
2.5ml/½ tsp vanilla extract
2 eggs, lightly beaten
gel or paste food colouring, red
15–30ml/1–2 tbsp milk

FOR THE DECORATION

40g/1½oz/3 tbsp butter, softened
115g/4oz/½ cup cream cheese, cold
250g/9oz/2¼ cups icing (confectioners') sugar, sifted
150g/5oz ready-to-roll fondant icing, white
gel or paste food colouring, black, blue
red food pen
15–30ml/1–2 tbsp seedless raspberry jam

➡ MAKES 12 CUPCAKES

Cook's Tips

Add the food colouring to the cake mixture before the flour. If you wait until after the flour has been folded in then you may end up over-mixing and the cakes will not rise as well.

1 Preheat the oven to 180°C/350°F/Gas 4. Line a muffin tin (pan) with cupcake cases. Sift the flour with the cocoa powder.

2 Cream the butter for a few minutes until soft and pale. Add the sugar and continue to beat until the mixture is pale and fluffy. Add the vanilla extract to the lightly beaten eggs, and then gradually add to the butter and sugar mixture, beating well between each addition. Add a teaspoonful of flour with the last two additions so that the mixture does not curdle. Add red food colouring, little by little, until the mixture is a strong red colour. Fold in the sifted flour and cocoa, add the milk, a little at a time, until the mixture drops slowly off the spoon.

3 Divide the mixture between the cupcake cases. Put in the oven and cook for 20–25 minutes until risen, lightly browned and bouncy to the touch. Allow to cool in the tin for a few minutes, then transfer to a wire rack, and allow to cool completely.

4 For the decoration, cream the butter for a few minutes until soft and pale. Drain the cream cheese and beat together with the butter until combined. Do not overbeat. Add half the sifted icing sugar and beat until combined, then beat in the remaining sugar. Chill until ready to use.

5 Colour a quarter of the ready-to-roll fondant icing pale grey with the black food colouring. Colour another quarter black. Create six grey blades with shafts, and moisten the shafts and wrap a little black icing around to make a handle – the knives should be about 6cm/2½in long in total. Set aside to dry (see p.151). Keep any leftover black icing.

6 To make the eyeballs, reserve a small ball of white ready-to-roll icing (about 10g/¼oz), then use the rest to roll three balls about 2.5cm/1in in diameter, and cut them in half. Colour the reserved ball blue with the food colouring, then roll it out and cut out six discs about 1cm/½in across. Roll out the leftover black icing and cut out six discs a little smaller than the blue discs. Moistening the undersides of the discs so that they stick, place one blue disc on the curved side of each white half-ball, and then top with a black disc. Draw veins on the whites of the eyeballs with the red food pen. Set aside to dry.

7 Pipe a shallow mound of icing on each cupcake with a large star nozzle, or swirl the icing with a knife. Add small blobs of jam for blood. Place the eyeballs and knives on the cupcakes.

Energy 348kcal/1461kJ; Protein 3g; Carbohydrate 50g, of which sugars 44g; Fat 17g, of which saturates 10g; Cholesterol 76mg; Calcium 49mg; Fibre 0g; Sodium 164mg

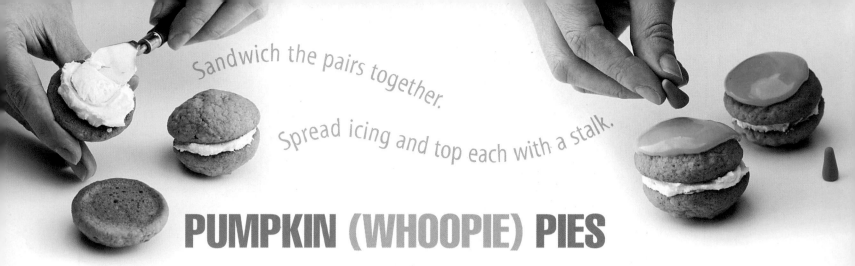

Sandwich the pairs together.

Spread icing and top each with a stalk.

PUMPKIN (WHOOPIE) PIES

Pumpkin whoopie pies, filled with cream cheese frosting and topped with glacé icing make a great treat for a Halloween party. If you are using canned pumpkin purée, make sure that you buy pure pumpkin – sometimes called 'solid pack' – rather than pumpkin pie filling which contains spices and sugar.

FOR THE CAKES
75g/3oz/6 tbsp butter
130g/4½oz/¾ cup soft light brown sugar
5ml/1 tsp vanilla extract
1 egg, lightly beaten
125g/4¼oz/½ cup unsweetened pumpkin purée
200g/7oz/1¾ cups self-raising (self-rising) flour
2.5ml/½ tsp baking powder
5ml/1 tsp ground cinnamon
2.5ml/½ tsp ground nutmeg (optional)
60ml/4 tbsp milk

FOR THE FILLING
40g/1½oz/3 tbsp butter, softened
115g/4oz/½ cup cream cheese, cold
250g/9oz/2¼ cups icing (confectioners') sugar, sifted

FOR THE DECORATION
40g/1½oz ready-to-roll fondant icing
gel or paste food colouring, green, orange
150g/5oz/1¼ cups icing (confectioners') sugar, sifted
30–40ml/2–2½ tbsp water or lemon juice

➤➤ MAKES 16 SMALL WHOOPIE PIES

1 Preheat the oven to 190°C/375°F/Gas 5. Line two large baking sheets with baking parchment.

2 Cream the butter for a few minutes until soft and pale. Add the sugar and continue to beat until the mixture is pale and fluffy. Add the vanilla extract to the lightly beaten egg and then gradually add to the butter and sugar mixture, beating well between each addition. Stir in the pumpkin purée. Don't worry if the mixture curdles. Sift the flour with the baking powder, cinnamon and nutmeg (if used) and stir into the mixture. Stir in the milk to loosen the mixture a little.

3 Using a teaspoon, spoon 16 rounds of mixture on each baking sheet – 32 in total. Use a wetted finger to smooth the tops (*see* p.151). Bake for 12–14 minutes until risen, lightly coloured and bouncy to the touch. Leave to cool on the baking sheets for a couple of minutes, then transfer to a wire rack to cool.

4 For the filling, cream the butter for a few minutes until soft and pale. Drain the cream cheese and beat together with the butter until combined. Do not overbeat. Add half the sifted icing sugar and beat until combined, then beat in the remaining sugar.

5 Match up the cakes for size and shape. Spread cream cheese filling on the flat side of half the cakes. Sandwich the pairs together.

6 Colour the ready-to-roll fondant icing green with food colouring. Shape 16 little green stalks. Set aside to dry.

7 Mix the icing sugar with water or lemon juice, 5ml/1 tsp at a time, until just thin enough to spread. Be cautious as the icing starts to reach the right consistency. Colour the icing orange. Spread icing on the filled pies and top each with a stalk.

Energy 277kcal/1166kJ; Protein 3g; Carbohydrate 47g, of which sugars 37g; Fat 10g, of which saturates 6g; Cholesterol 53mg; Calcium 70mg; Fibre 1g; Sodium 144mg

TOFFEE APPLE CUPCAKES

Variations

This recipe also works well with other firm fruit such as chopped fresh peach, plum or apricot.

Fresh chunks of apple are the surprise inside these caramel-topped cupcakes. We like to make them for fireworks parties or Halloween treats. Children will love to watch the mini sparklers, but make sure that they keep well back.

FOR THE CAKES

115g/4oz/½ cup butter
150g/5oz/¾ cup caster (superfine) sugar
2.5ml/½ tsp vanilla extract
2 eggs, lightly beaten
150g/5oz/1½ cups self-raising (self-rising) flour, sifted
a pinch of salt
30–45ml/2–3 tbsp milk
1 eating apple

FOR THE DECORATION

50g/2oz/¼ cup butter
90g/3½oz/generous ½ cup soft dark brown sugar
a pinch of salt
30ml/2 tbsp milk
2.5ml/½ tsp vanilla extract
90g/3½oz/¾ cup icing (confectioners') sugar, sifted
gold sugar stars
edible gold glitter
12 mini sparklers or gold candles

▶▶ MAKES 12 CUPCAKES

Decorate with gold stars and mini sparklers …

1 Preheat the oven to 180°C/350°F/Gas 4. Line a muffin tin (pan) with cupcake cases.

2 Cream the butter for a few minutes until soft and pale. Add the sugar and continue to beat until the mixture is pale and fluffy.

3 Add the vanilla extract to the lightly beaten eggs and then gradually add to the butter and sugar mixture, beating well between each addition. Add a teaspoonful of flour with the last two additions, so that the mixture does not curdle.

4 Fold in the sifted flour with the salt and then add the milk, a little at a time, until the mixture drops slowly off the spoon.

5 Peel, core and chop the apple into small pieces (about 5mm/¼in). Fold into the mixture (*see* p.151).

6 Divide the mixture between the cupcake cases. Bake for 20–25 minutes until risen, lightly browned and bouncy to the touch. Take the cakes out of the oven, leave in the tin for a few minutes, then transfer to a wire rack to cool completely.

7 For the caramel decoration, put the butter, soft dark brown sugar and salt in a small pan and stir over a low heat until the sugar has dissolved. Add the milk and vanilla extract, and bring to the boil. Boil for 3 minutes, stirring occasionally. Remove from the heat add the icing sugar, then whisk until smooth.

8 Allow the caramel to cool a little until it starts to thicken, then spread on the cupcakes. If the caramel hardens too much, just reheat it.

9 Decorate with gold stars, glitter and mini sparklers or candles.

Energy 272kcal/1144kJ; Protein 3g; Carbohydrate 40g, of which sugars 30g; Fat 13g, of which saturates 8g; Cholesterol 70mg; Calcium 65mg; Fibre 1g; Sodium 124mg

Children will love to
watch the mini sparklers ...

Sometimes only a cupcake will do for a celebration. Italian meringue frosting coloured very pale blue sparkles with stars, sprinkles and candles. The frosting is easy to make and produces a shiny, fluffy topping. Sugar syrup is beaten into egg whites and, if you prefer, this recipe can be made using reconstituted pasteurized dried egg white powder or pasteurized carton egg whites. Alternatively you could use buttercream. This frosting is best eaten on the day it is made.

WELL DONE!

FOR THE CAKES
115g/4oz/½ cup butter
115g/4oz/generous ½ cup caster (superfine) sugar
5ml/1 tsp vanilla extract
2 eggs, lightly beaten
115g/4oz/1 cup self-raising (self-rising) flour, sifted
15–30ml/1–2 tbsp milk

➡ **MAKES 12 CUPCAKES**

FOR THE DECORATION
115g/4oz/generous ½ cup caster (superfine) sugar
90ml/6 tbsp water
2 egg whites
gel or paste food colouring, blue
edible stars
silver and pearl sprinkles
12 candles

1 Preheat the oven to 180°C/350°F/Gas 4. Line a muffin tin (pan) with cupcake cases.

2 Cream the butter for a few minutes until soft and pale. Add the sugar and continue to beat until the mixture is pale and fluffy.

3 Add the vanilla extract to the lightly beaten eggs and then gradually add to the butter and sugar mixture, beating well between each addition. Add a teaspoonful of flour with the last two additions, so that the mixture does not curdle.

4 Fold in the sifted flour and then add the milk, a little at a time, until the mixture drops slowly off the spoon.

5 Divide the mixture between the cupcake cases. Bake for 20–25 minutes until risen, lightly browned and bouncy to the touch. Take the cakes out of the oven, leave in the tin for a few minutes, then transfer to a wire rack to cool completely.

6 For the decoration, place the sugar and water in a small heavy pan and heat gently until the sugar has completely dissolved. Wipe away any sugar crystals on the side of the pan with a pastry brush dipped in water. Increase the heat and boil without stirring until the temperature of the mixture reaches 119°C/238°F on a sugar thermometer (or a small amount of syrup dropped into a glass of cold water forms a soft ball).

7 Beat the egg whites with an electric whisk until they stand in soft peaks. Pouring the syrup down the side of the bowl and beating all the time, whisk until the mixture is stiff and glossy (*see* p.151). Beat in a few drops of blue food colouring to colour the icing pale blue, then spoon the mixture into a piping (pastry) bag with a large star nozzle. Pipe shallow mounds on the cupcakes.

8 Decorate with stars and sprinkles, and stick a candle on the top of each cupcake.

Energy 196kcal/822kJ; Protein 3g; Carbohydrate 28g, of which sugars 20g; Fat 9g, of which saturates 5g; Cholesterol 60mg; Calcium 45mg; Fibre 0g; Sodium 119mg

STORY
Time

Everyone has
their favourite
superhero.

The Queen of Hearts would love these cakes.

TEDDY BEARS' PICNIC CUPCAKES

... weave into a mat and pipe grass on the cupcakes.

Bears love honey and so we made honey cupcakes for a teddy bears' picnic.

Use a strong honey, if possible, to get the best flavour. Picnic rugs for the bears are woven with roll-out icing and then cut into circles to make little individual mats for the teddy bears. Just a small amount of honey in the icing gives a distinct honey taste, but if you prefer, flavour the icing by using lemon juice instead of milk.

FOR THE CAKES
115g/4oz/½ cup butter
50g/2oz/generous ¼ cup caster (superfine) sugar
65g/2½oz/¼ cup honey
2 eggs, lightly beaten
115g/4oz/1 cup self-raising (self-rising) flour, sifted
15–30ml/1–2 tbsp milk

FOR THE DECORATION
400g/14oz ready-to-roll fondant icing
gel or paste food colouring, blue, pink, brown, bright green
115g/4oz/½ cup butter, softened
225g/8oz/2 cups icing (confectioners') sugar, sifted
2.5ml/½ tsp honey (optional)
5–10ml/1–2 tsp milk

▶▶ MAKES 12 CUPCAKES

1 Preheat the oven to 180°C/350°F/Gas 4. Line a muffin tin (pan) with cupcake cases.

2 Cream the butter for a few minutes until soft and pale. Add the sugar and honey, and continue to beat until the mixture is pale and fluffy.

3 Gradually add the lightly beaten eggs to the butter mixture, beating well between each addition. Add a teaspoonful of flour with the last two additions, so that the mixture does not curdle.

4 Fold in the sifted flour and then add the milk, a little at a time, until the mixture drops slowly off the spoon.

5 Divide the mixture between the cupcake cases. Bake for 20–25 minutes until risen, lightly browned and bouncy to the touch. Allow the cakes to cool in the tin for a few minutes, then transfer to a wire rack to cool completely.

6 For the decoration, colour one quarter of the ready-to-roll fondant icing pale blue, one quarter pale pink and the remaining half brown. Roll thin strands of pink and blue icing and weave into a mat (*see* p.151). You will probably find it easiest to do this in several smaller mats rather than trying to make one huge mat. Gently roll over the mat with a rolling pin so that the strands bind together. Cut out 12 circles about 4cm/1½in across. Model 12 mini teddy bears with the brown icing. Press marks for eyes with a skewer or a cocktail stick (toothpick). Set aside to dry.

7 Cream the butter until soft and pale. Gradually add the sifted icing sugar, beating well between each addition. Beat in the honey (if used) and then colour the icing grass green with the food colouring. Pipe grass on the cupcakes with a small star nozzle and place a picnic mat and a teddy on top of each cupcake.

Energy 411kcal/1729kJ; Protein 3g; Carbohydrate 66g, of which sugars 58g; Fat 17g, of which saturates 10g; Cholesterol 81mg; Calcium 49mg; Fibre 0g; Sodium 179mg

FAIRY PRINCESS
CUPCAKES

Variations

Instead of using freeze-dried raspberries, put 2.5ml/½ tsp of raspberry jam in the middle of the cake mixture.

There's a delicious raspberry surprise inside these perfectly girly cupcakes, and this is the moment to let your inner princess loose with crowns, sugar pearls, glitter and sugar flowers. We have made lavender-coloured buttercream, but it could, of course, be pink.

FOR THE CAKES

115g/4oz/½ cup butter
115g/4oz/generous ½ cup caster (superfine) sugar
5ml/1 tsp vanilla extract
2 eggs, lightly beaten
115g/4oz/1 cup self-raising (self-rising) flour, sifted
8–10g/4 tbsp freeze-dried raspberries, crumbled if whole
15–30ml/1–2 tbsp milk

➡ MAKES 12 CUPCAKES

FOR THE DECORATION

115g/4oz ready-to-roll fondant icing
gel or paste food colouring, yellow, purple
writing icing, red or white
115g/4oz/½ cup butter, softened
225g/8oz/2 cups icing (confectioners') sugar, sifted
5–10ml/1–2 tsp lemon juice
small sugar flowers
edible sugar pearls
edible glitter

1 Preheat the oven to 180°C/350°F/Gas 4. Line a muffin tin (pan) with cupcake cases.

2 Cream the butter for a few minutes until soft and pale. Add the sugar and continue to beat until the mixture is pale and fluffy. Add the vanilla extract to the lightly beaten eggs and then gradually add to the butter and sugar mixture, beating well between each addition. Add a teaspoonful of flour with the last two additions, so that the mixture does not curdle. Fold in the sifted flour and the freeze-dried raspberries (*see* p.152), then add the milk, a little at a time until the mixture drops slowly off the spoon.

3 Divide the mixture between the cupcake cases. Bake for 20–25 minutes until risen, lightly browned and bouncy to the touch. Allow the cakes to cool in the tin for a few minutes, then transfer to a wire rack to cool completely.

4 To make the crowns, colour the ready-to-roll fondant icing yellow with the gel food colouring. Roll out and cut strips about 7.5cm/3in long by 2.5cm/1in deep. Cut points along one edge and then join the short ends together to make a crown. Curve out the points. Decorate the points with a blob of red writing icing or fix a sugar pearl in place on each point with a little dot of writing icing. Set aside to dry.

5 Cream the butter until soft and pale. Gradually add the sifted icing sugar, beating well between each addition. Beat in the lemon juice to make the icing just soft enough to pipe.

6 Colour the buttercream pale lavender with a few drops of purple food colouring. Pipe a shallow mound of buttercream on each cupcake with a large star nozzle. Top each cupcake with a crown and then decorate the cakes with sugar flowers and pearls, and dust with glitter.

Energy 269kcal/1125kJ; Protein 2g; Carbohydrate 29g,
of which sugars 21g; Fat 17g, of which saturates 10g;
Cholesterol 81mg; Calcium 47mg; Fibre 1g; Sodium 169mg

SLEEPING BEAUTY TOWERS

These pretty fairy-tale towers have been made in individual pudding moulds. You could also use dariole moulds which are traditionally used for making English madeleine cakes and would give the towers a little extra height. The cake is flavoured with rose water, but you could use vanilla extract instead.

FOR THE CAKES
115g/4oz/½ cup butter
115g/4oz/generous ½ cup caster (superfine) sugar
2.5–5ml/½–1 tsp rose water
2 eggs, lightly beaten
115g/4oz/1 cup self-raising (self-rising) flour, sifted
15–30ml/1–2 tbsp milk

➡ **MAKES 12 CUPCAKES**

FOR THE DECORATION
175g/6oz ready-to-roll fondant icing, white
gel or paste food colouring, pink, green, red
175g/6oz/1½ cups icing (confectioners') sugar
¾ egg white (about 25g/1oz/1½ tbsp)
5ml/1 tsp glycerine
5ml/1 tsp lemon juice (optional)
5–10ml/1–2 tsp water
12 paper flags

Cook's Tips
Use a broad palette knife to lift the cakes off the rack and on to serving plates. The moulds we used are about 75ml/7 tbsp in volume. If your moulds are larger then you will make fewer cakes.

1 Preheat the oven to 180°C/350°F/Gas 4. Thoroughly grease the moulds and dust with flour – this will make all the difference to turning out the cakes. Stand them on a baking tray or in a muffin tin (pan).

2 Cream the butter for a few minutes until soft and pale. Add the sugar and continue to beat until the mixture is pale and fluffy. Add the rose water to the lightly beaten eggs and then gradually add to the butter and sugar mixture, beating well between each addition. Add a teaspoonful of flour with the last two additions, so that the mixture does not curdle. Fold in the sifted flour and then add the milk, a little at a time, until the mixture drops slowly off the spoon.

3 Divide the mixture between the moulds. Bake for 25 minutes until risen, lightly browned and bouncy to the touch. Allow the cakes to cool in the moulds for a few minutes, then transfer to a wire rack to cool completely.

4 For the decoration, colour the ready-to-roll fondant icing dark pink with food colouring. Roll out the icing to 3–5mm/⅛–¼in thick and cut a circle about 10cm/4in across. Cut the circle into thirds. Moisten the long straight edge of one third and wrap around to make a cone, sticking the long side together. Adjust the base so that it will fit on top of the cakes. Do the same with the other thirds and continue rolling out and cutting to make nine other cones. Set aside to dry.

5 Sift the icing sugar and set aside. Beat the egg white until frothy and then gradually add the sugar, beating until the mixture is thick and glossy. Add the glycerine and lemon juice (if used) and continue beating until the mixture is thick and very white and forms pointy peaks. This will take at least 5 minutes with an electric whisk.

6 Reserve about 45ml/3tbsp icing and cover tightly. Stir 5ml/1 tsp water into the remaining icing and test the texture by drawing a knife through the icing and then counting how long the mark takes to fill in. Add a little more water if necessary until the mark fills in after a steady count of 15. Colour the icing pale pink.

7 Trim a little off the cakes so that they stand flat upside down. Rub off any loose crumbs and place the cakes on a rack with a large plate underneath to catch drops of icing. Spoon icing over each cupcake and spread it over the sides, holding it in your fingers if necessary (*see* p.152). Top each cake with a pink cone and set aside to set for 30 minutes.

8 Colour half the reserved royal icing green and the other half red. Using a small plain icing nozzle pipe green tendrils over the towers. Then using a small star nozzle pipe little red roses. Stick a flag in the top of each roof.

Energy 264kcal/1115kJ; Protein 3g; Carbohydrate 46g, of which sugars 39g; Fat 9g, of which saturates 5g; Cholesterol 60mg; Calcium 46mg; Fibre 0g; Sodium 118mg

PIRATE CUPCAKES

All set for a jolly pirate party? Juicy lemon and raisin cupcakes are topped with royal icing and shapes cut out of ready-to-roll fondant icing. We have had fun with pirate faces and skulls and crossbones, but you could try pirate hats, hooks, cutlasses and even the odd parrot or two.

FOR THE CAKES

115g/4oz/½ cup butter
115g/4oz/generous ½ cup caster (superfine) sugar
2 eggs, lightly beaten
115g/4oz/1 cup self-raising (self-rising) flour, sifted
grated rind of 1 lemon
75g/3oz/½ cup raisins
15–30ml/1–2 tbsp lemon juice

➡➡ MAKES 12 CUPCAKES

FOR THE DECORATION

115g/4oz/1 cup icing (confectioners') sugar
½ egg white (about 17g/½oz/generous 1 tbsp)
2.5ml/½ tsp glycerine
2.5ml/½ tsp lemon juice (optional)
5–7.5 ml/1–1½ tsp water
250g/9oz ready-to-roll fondant icing, white
gel or paste food colouring, black, blue
writing icing, black and red

1 Preheat the oven to 180°C/350°F/Gas 4. Line a muffin tin (pan) with cupcake cases.

2 Cream the butter for a few minutes until soft and pale. Add the sugar and continue to beat until the mixture is pale and fluffy. Gradually add the lightly beaten eggs to the butter and sugar mixture, beating well between each addition. Add a teaspoonful of flour with each of the last two additions, so that the mixture does not curdle. Fold in the sifted flour, the grated rind and the raisins, then add the lemon juice, as little at a time, until the mixture drops slowly off the spoon.

3 Divide the mixture between the cupcake cases. Bake for 20–25 minutes until risen, lightly browned and bouncy to the touch. Allow the cakes to cool in the tin for a few minutes, then transfer to a wire rack to cool completely.

4 Sift the icing sugar and set aside. Beat the egg white until frothy and then gradually add the sugar, beating until the mixture is thick and glossy. Add the glycerine and lemon juice (if using), and continue beating until the mixture is thick and very white and forms pointy peaks. This will take at least 5 minutes with an electric whisk.

5 Put a tablespoon of icing in a piping (pastry) bag with a small round piping nozzle. Stir 5ml/1 tsp water into the rest of the icing and test the texture by drawing a knife through the icing and then counting how long the mark takes to fill in. Add a little more water if necessary until you reach the point where the mark fills in after a steady count of 15. Spread icing on the cupcakes.

6 Colour half of the ready-to-roll fondant icing black and half bright blue. Roll lengths of black icing and shape into bones. Cut out six skulls – we find it easiest to cut circles with a small circular cutter and then shape (*see* p.152). Cut out the eyes, nose and mouth. Arrange the skulls and crossbones on six of the cupcakes. Reserve the remaining black icing.

7 Roll out the blue icing and cut out three circles the size of the top of the cupcakes, then cut in half for the pirates' scarves. Cut six eye patches and roll six moustaches from the remaining black icing and set aside. Assemble the pirate faces and pipe white spots on the scarves with white icing in the piping bag. Add eyes and eye-patch strings with the black icing and mouths with red icing.

Energy 282kcal/1189kJ; Protein 3g; Carbohydrate 51g, of which sugars 43g; Fat 9g, of which saturates 5g; Cholesterol 60mg; Calcium 47mg; Fibre 1g; Sodium 118mg

SECRET TREASURE WHOOPIE PIES

Spread sprinkles, pearls, gold flakes and jelly sweets.

Gold and silver pirate treasure resting on a bed of white chocolate buttercream peeps out from inside chocolate shells, just waiting to be discovered. We used a selection of gold, silver and bronze sprinkles, edible pearls and a few yellow jellied sweets.

FOR THE CAKES
75g/3oz/6 tbsp butter
130g/4½oz/¾ cup soft light brown sugar
5ml/1 tsp vanilla extract
1 egg, lightly beaten
175g/6oz/1½ cups self-raising (self-rising) flour
2.5ml/½ tsp baking powder
25g/1oz/¼ cup unsweetened cocoa powder
120ml/4fl oz/½ cup milk

▶▶ MAKES 16 SMALL WHOOPIE PIES

FOR THE DECORATION
50g/2oz white chocolate
115g/4oz/½ cup butter, softened
225g/8oz/2 cups icing (confectioners') sugar, sifted
5–10ml/1–2 tsp milk
selection of gold, silver and bronze sprinkles and dragées
edible pearls
gold flakes
yellow and orange jellied sweets
 (candies)

1 Preheat the oven to 190°C/375°F/Gas 5. Line two large baking sheets with baking parchment.

2 Cream the butter for a few minutes until soft and pale. Add the sugar and continue to beat until the mixture is pale and fluffy.

3 Add the vanilla extract to the lightly beaten egg and then gradually add to the butter and sugar mixture, beating well between each addition.

4 Sift the flour with the baking powder and cocoa. Stir half the flour into the mixture, then stir in half the milk. Stir in the remaining flour and then the remaining milk until the mixture is well combined, but don't over mix.

5 Using a teaspoon, spoon 16 rounds of mixture on each baking sheet – 32 in total. Bake for 10–12 minutes, until risen and bouncy to the touch. Allow to cool on the baking sheets for a couple of minutes, then transfer the cakes to a rack to cool.

6 For the decoration, melt the chocolate in a microwave or in a bowl over a pan of gently simmering water. Set aside to cool.

7 Cream the butter until soft and pale. Gradually add the sifted icing sugar, beating well between each addition. Beat in the cooled, melted chocolate (*see* p.152) and then add the milk, if necessary, a little at a time, to make the icing just soft enough to pipe.

8 Match up the cakes for size and shape. Pipe buttercream on the flat side of half the cakes using a large star piping nozzle or spread the buttercream. Spread sprinkles, pearls, gold flakes and jellied sweets on one side of the cakes, then place the other cakes at an angle on top so that they look like an oyster shell just opening to reveal the treasure.

Energy 240kcal/1006kJ; Protein 2g; Carbohydrate 34g, of which sugars 25g; Fat 12g, of which saturates 7g; Cholesterol 41mg; Calcium 68mg; Fibre 0g; Sodium 157mg

SUPERHERO CUPCAKES

Everyone has their favourite superhero. We have made simple blue, red and yellow masks, but you can always use the same technique to make your favourite character's mask.

FOR THE CAKES
115g/4oz/½ cup butter
115g/4oz/generous ½ cup caster (superfine) sugar
5ml/1 tsp vanilla extract
2 eggs, lightly beaten
115g/4oz/1 cup self-raising (self-rising) flour, sifted
15–30ml/1–2 tbsp milk

➡➡ **MAKES 12 CUPCAKES**

FOR THE DECORATION
115g/4oz/1 cup icing (confectioners') sugar
½ egg white (about 17g/½oz/generous 1 tbsp)
2.5ml/½ tsp glycerine
2.5ml/½ tsp lemon juice (optional)
5–7.5ml/1–1½ tsp water
gel or paste food colouring, yellow, light
  blue, green, dark blue, red
175g/6oz ready-to-roll fondant icing, white

1 Preheat the oven to 180°C/350°F/Gas 4. Line a muffin tin (pan) with cupcake cases.

2 Cream the butter for a few minutes until soft and pale. Add the sugar and continue to beat until the mixture is pale and fluffy.

3 Add the vanilla extract to the lightly beaten eggs and then gradually add to the butter and sugar mixture, beating well between each addition. Add a teaspoon of flour with the last two additions so that the mixture does not curdle.

4 Fold in the sifted flour and then add the milk, a little at a time, until the mixture drops slowly off the spoon.

5 Divide the mixture between the cupcake cases. Bake for 20–25 minutes until risen, lightly browned and bouncy to the touch. Allow the cakes to cool in the tin for a few minutes, then transfer to a wire rack to cool completely.

6 For the decoration, sift the icing sugar and set aside. Beat the egg white until frothy and then gradually add the sugar, beating until the mixture is thick and glossy. Add the glycerine and lemon juice (if used), and continue beating until the mixture is thick and very white and forms pointy peaks when you lift the whisk. This will take at least 5 minutes with an electric whisk.

7 Stir 5ml/1 tsp water into the icing and test the texture by drawing a knife through the icing and then counting how long the mark takes to fill in. Add a little more water if necessary until you reach the point where the mark fills in after a steady count of 15. Divide the icing into three. Colour one portion yellow, one portion light blue and the remaining portion green (*see* p.152). Use each colour to ice four cupcakes.

8 Divide the ready-to-roll fondant icing into three pieces with one piece slightly smaller than the other. Colour the smaller piece dark blue, and the other two pieces yellow and red. Roll out and cut four masks from the dark blue icing. Roll out the red icing and cut four masks, four small stars and eight lightning bolts. Roll out the yellow icing and cut four masks, eight small stars and four lightning bolts.

9 Position the masks on contrasting cupcakes and decorate with stars and lightning bolts.

Energy 244kcal/1030kJ; Protein 2g; Carbohydrate 41g, of which sugars 33g; Fat 9g, of which saturates 5g; Cholesterol 60mg; Calcium 45mg; Fibre 0g; Sodium 116mg

ALIEN MONSTER POPS

Cook's Tips

It is essential to have either some polystyrene (Styrofoam) or blocks of florists' form to stick the pop sticks in as the decorations set.

Dip a whole cake pop in the green covering and decorate.

These extra-terrestrial pops are a great opportunity to try out weird combinations of bright colours, bulging eyes, and scary horns and teeth. Ready-coloured chocolate buttons or candy melts (which you can get from specialist cake decorating shops or in online stores) give the strongest colours and we have used them here, but you can use white chocolate and colour it with gel or paste food colouring if you prefer.

FOR THE CAKE POPS

25g/1oz plain (semisweet) chocolate
65g/2½oz/5 tbsp butter, softened
150g/5oz/1¼ cups icing (confectioners') sugar, sifted
5–10ml/1–2 tsp milk
375g–400g/13–14oz chocolate cake
  (*see* recipe p.16 or use store-bought)

➡ MAKES 20–24 CAKE POPS

FOR THE DECORATION

200g/7oz ready-to-roll fondant icing, white
50g/2oz ready-to-roll fondant icing, black
gel or paste food colouring, blue
300g/10oz green candy melts or coloured chocolate buttons
50g/2oz yellow candy melts or coloured chocolate buttons
10–15ml/2–3 tsp vegetable oil (optional)
24 cake pop sticks

1 Melt the chocolate in a microwave or in a bowl over a pan of gently simmering water. Set aside to cool.

2 Cream the butter until soft and pale. Gradually add the sifted icing sugar, beating well between each addition. Beat in the cooled, melted chocolate. Add the milk, a little at a time, if the icing is very stiff.

3 Crumble the cake into fine crumbs (this is easiest to do in a food processor), and put the crumbs in a large bowl. Mix in the buttercream, a spoonful at a time. The mixture needs to bind together and be mouldable but not too wet. You may not need all the buttercream. Shape the mixture into balls weighing about 25g/1oz each. Chill the balls for at least 30 minutes until firm but not completely solid.

4 Take half the white ready-to-roll fondant icing and make at least 40 balls about 1cm/½in across for eyes. Make smaller balls from the black icing and press on to the white balls. Colour half the remaining white icing blue and make horns. Cut teeth from the remaining white icing (*see* p.153).

5 Melt the green covering in a microwave oven or in a bowl over a pan of gently simmering water. Dip a stick in the covering and then insert it about halfway into a ball. Repeat with the remaining balls and, if necessary, chill until firm. Melt the yellow covering.

6 Dip a whole cake pop in the green covering, using a spoon if necessary to help with covering the cake. If the covering is too thick, thin with a little vegetable oil (not water). Gently tap and twirl to shake off excess. Rough up the surface with the back of a teaspoon. Press on eyes, horns and teeth and drop on spots of yellow. Stick the pop into a block of polystyrene (Styrofoam) or florists' foam and leave to dry or chill. Repeat with the rest of the pops.

Energy 217kcal/913kJ; Protein 2g; Carbohydrate 31g, of which sugars 25g; Fat 10g, of which saturates 6g; Cholesterol 38mg; Calcium 39mg; Fibre 0g; Sodium 90mg

Bright colours, bulging eyes, and scary horns and teeth.

CARS AND TRUCKS CUPCAKES

Some children just love moving vehicles of all kinds. We have made cars and trucks, but you can experiment with diggers, ambulances, fire vehicles – whatever your child loves most. For a birthday pipe your child's age on the top of each vehicle in a contrasting colour.

FOR THE CAKES
115g/4oz/½ cup butter
115g/4oz/generous ½ cup caster (superfine) sugar
2 eggs, lightly beaten
115g/4oz/1 cup self-raising (self-rising) flour, sifted
grated rind of 1 orange
15–30ml/1–2 tbsp orange juice

➡ **MAKES 12 CUPCAKES**

FOR THE DECORATION
115g/4oz/1 cup icing (confectioners') sugar
½ egg white (about 17g/½oz/generous 1 tbsp)
2.5ml/½ tsp glycerine
5ml/1 tsp lemon juice (optional)
5–7.5ml/1–1½ tsp water
gel or paste food colouring, black, blue, red,
   yellow, green and pink
250g/9oz ready-to-roll fondant icing, white

1 Preheat the oven to 180°C/350°F/Gas 4. Line a muffin tin (pan) with cupcake cases.

2 Cream the butter for a few minutes until soft and pale. Add the sugar and continue to beat until the mixture is pale and fluffy. Gradually add the lightly beaten eggs to the butter and sugar mixture, beating well between each addition. Add a teaspoonful of flour with each of the last two additions, so that the mixture does not curdle. Fold in the sifted flour and the grated rind, then add the orange juice, a little at a time, until the mixture drops slowly off the spoon.

3 Divide the mixture between the cupcake cases. Bake for 20–25 minutes until risen, lightly browned and bouncy to the touch. Allow to cool in the tin for a couple of minutes, then transfer to a wire rack to cool completely.

4 For the decoration, sift the icing sugar and set aside. Beat the egg white until frothy and then gradually add the sugar, beating until the mixture is thick and glossy. Add the glycerine and lemon juice (if used), and continue beating until the mixture is thick and very white and forms pointy peaks when you lift the whisk. This will take at least 5 minutes with an electric whisk.

5 Reserve 15ml/1 tbsp of icing and cover. Stir 5ml/1 tsp water into the remaining icing and test the texture by drawing a knife through the icing and then counting how long the mark takes to fill in. Add a little more water if necessary until you reach the point where the mark fills in after a steady count of 15. Colour the icing a grey/blue colour with food colouring. Ice the cupcakes.

6 Reserve a walnut-sized piece of the white ready-to-roll fondant icing and then divide the rest into six and colour the portions red, blue, yellow, green, pink and black with food colouring. Set the black portion aside, and use the other colours to create various car and truck shapes. Form wheels for the trucks and the cars from the black icing. Roll the reserved white icing out thinly and cut windscreens and stick on to the vehicles. Mark lines on the wheels for sports cars, or add white centres for large truck wheels (*see* p.153). Add headlights with tiny pieces of white or yellow icing.

7 Position one of the vehicles on top of each cupcake and pipe road markings with the remaining reserved white icing using a fine piping nozzle.

Energy 266kcal/1121kJ; Protein 3g; Carbohydrate 46g, of which sugars 39g; Fat 9g, of which saturates 5g;
Cholesterol 60mg; Calcium 44mg; Fibre 0g; Sodium 117mg

Cook's Tips

For the best effect, mix the
pink and white mixtures
in the cupcake cases
very lightly.

MAGICAL SWEETSHOP CUPCAKES

Bite into these cupcakes and you will find pretty pink-and-white marbled sponge.
Be bold with the pink colouring – the effect is always less than you expect when the cakes are
cooked. Choose a selection of your favourite old-fashioned sweets to decorate – jellies,
candy-coated chocolates, sherbets – and top with a lollipop or candy cane.

FOR THE CAKES
115g/4oz/½ cup butter
115g/4oz/generous ½ cup caster (superfine) sugar
5ml/1 tsp vanilla extract
2 eggs, lightly beaten
115g/4oz/1 cup self-raising (self-rising) flour, sifted
15–30ml/1–2 tbsp milk
gel or paste food colouring, pink

➡ **MAKES 12 CUPCAKES**

FOR THE DECORATION
115g/4oz/½ cup butter, softened
225g/8oz/2 cups icing (confectioners')
 sugar, sifted
5ml/1 tsp vanilla extract
5–10ml/1–2 tsp milk
gel or paste food colouring, pink
about 175g/6oz mixed colourful old-fashioned
 sweets (candies)
12 small candy canes or whirly lollipops
coloured sugar sprinkles or edible glitter

1 Preheat the oven to 180°C/350°F/Gas 4. Line a muffin tin (pan) with cupcake cases.

2 Cream the butter for a few minutes until soft and pale. Add the sugar and continue to beat until
the mixture is pale and fluffy. Add the vanilla extract to the lightly beaten eggs and then gradually
add to the butter and sugar mixture, beating well between each addition. Add a teaspoonful of flour with
the last two additions, so that the mixture does not curdle. Fold in the sifted flour and then add the milk,
a little at a time, until the mixture drops slowly off the spoon.

3 Spoon half the mixture into another bowl and colour a strong pink with the food colouring (*see* p.153).
Using a teaspoon, put a spoonful of pink mixture in each cupcake case, followed by a spoonful of plain mixture.
Continue until the mixture is used up. Then use a toothpick (cocktail stick) or a skewer to lightly swirl the
mixture together. Bake for 20–25 minutes until risen, lightly browned and bouncy to the touch. Allow
the cakes to cool in the tin for a few minutes, then transfer to a wire rack to cool completely.

4 For the decoration, cream the butter until soft and pale. Gradually add the sifted icing sugar, beating well
between each addition. Beat in the vanilla extract and then add enough of the milk to make the icing just soft
enough to pipe. Colour the mixture pale pink with the food colouring. Pipe or swirl the icing on the
cupcakes, then decorate with sweets, and top with a candy cane or lollipop and a pinch of sugar
sprinkles or edible glitter.

Energy 319kcal/1464kJ; Protein 3g; Carbohydrate 49g, of which sugars 38g; Fat 17g, of which saturates 10g;
Cholesterol 81mg; Calcium 48mg; Fibre 0g; Sodium 173mg

Wizard hats glittering on top of chocolate cupcakes are perfect for a magical party, and chocolate matchsticks make excellent miniature wands. Dark cases produce the best effect with matching hats. We found dark blue cases, but dark purple or green would also look good.

WIZARD'S HAT CUPCAKES

Shape one quarter
into a tall narrow cone.

FOR THE CAKES

90g/3½oz/¾ cup self-raising (self-rising) flour
25g/1oz/¼ cup unsweetened cocoa powder
115g/4oz/½ cup butter
115g/4oz/scant ¾ cup soft light brown sugar
2 eggs, lightly beaten
15–30ml/1–2 tbsp milk

▶▶ **MAKES 12 CUPCAKES**

FOR THE DECORATION

175g/6oz ready-to-roll fondant icing, white
gel or paste food colouring, blue
50g/2oz plain (semisweet) chocolate
115g/4oz/½ cup butter, softened
225g/8oz/2 cups icing (confectioners') sugar, sifted
5–10ml/1–2 tsp milk
gold edible glitter
12 short or 6 long chocolate matchsticks

1 Preheat the oven to 180°C/350°F/Gas 4. Line a muffin tin (pan) with cupcake cases.

2 Sift together the flour and the cocoa, and set aside. Cream the butter for a few minutes until soft and pale. Add the sugar and continue to beat until the mixture is pale and fluffy.

3 Gradually add the lightly beaten eggs to the butter and sugar mixture, beating well between each addition. Add a teaspoonful of flour with each of the last two additions so that the mixture does not curdle.

4 Fold in the sifted flour and cocoa and then add the milk, a little at a time, until the mixture drops slowly off the spoon. Divide the mixture between the cupcake cases. Bake for 20–25 minutes until risen, lightly browned and bouncy to the touch. Allow the cakes to cool in the tin for a few minutes, then transfer to a wire rack to cool completely.

5 For the decoration, colour the ready-to-roll fondant icing blue with the food colouring. Divide the icing into three pieces. Take one piece, roll out to about 3mm/⅛in thick, cut out a 10cm/4in circle and cut the circle into quarters. Shape one quarter into a tall narrow cone (*see* p.153), pressing the long edges together, and then press the base out into a brim. Repeat with the other quarters and the remaining pieces of icing. Set aside to dry.

6 Melt the chocolate in a microwave or in a bowl over a pan of gently simmering water. Set aside to cool.

7 Cream the butter until soft and pale. Gradually add the sifted icing sugar, beating well between each addition. Beat in the cooled, melted chocolate and then add the milk, if necessary, to make the icing just soft enough to pipe.

8 Pipe swirls of buttercream on the cakes using a large star piping nozzle. Place a hat on top of each cake and sprinkle with edible glitter. Add a chocolate matchstick (or half, if the matchsticks are long) as a wand to each cake.

Energy 396kcal/1661kJ; Protein 3g; Carbohydrate 53g, of which sugars 47g; Fat 21g, of which saturates 13g; Cholesterol 81mg; Calcium 61mg; Fibre 0g; Sodium 178mg

Place a hat on top of each cake and sprinkle with edible glitter.

QUEEN OF HEARTS ♥
MINI SANDWICH CAKES

The Queen of Hearts from Alice in Wonderland would be delighted to have these heart-shaped Victoria sponges at her croquet party. It is possible to get mats or textured rolling pins to produce a textured finish to the ready-to-roll fondant icing, but we have found lots of things around the house that can be used to produce a pretty texture.

FOR THE CAKES
115g/4oz/½ cup butter
115g/4oz/generous ½ cup caster (superfine) sugar
2 eggs, lightly beaten
115g/4oz/1 cup self-raising (self-rising) flour, sifted
grated rind of 1 lemon
15–30ml/1–2 tbsp lemon juice

FOR THE DECORATION
50g/2oz ready-to-roll fondant icing, red
a piece of light card
about 90g/3½oz/⅓ cup raspberry jam
150g/5oz/1¼ cups icing (confectioners') sugar, sifted
15–30ml/1–2 tbsp lemon juice
edible glitter (optional)

■➤ MAKES 8 MINI SANDWICH CAKES

1 Preheat the oven to 180°C/350°F/Gas 4. Lightly grease a 8-cup heart-shaped silicone mould and dust with flour. Stand the mould on a baking sheet.

2 Cream the butter for a few minutes until soft and pale. Add the sugar and continue to beat until the mixture is pale and fluffy. Gradually add the lightly beaten eggs to the butter and sugar mixture, beating well between each addition. Add a teaspoonful of flour with each of the last two additions, so that the mixture does not curdle. Fold in the sifted flour and the grated rind, then add the juice, a little at a time, until the mixture drops slowly off the spoon.

3 Divide the mixture between the moulds, filling to about half to two-thirds full. Bake for 20–25 minutes until risen, lightly browned and bouncy to the touch. Allow to cool in the moulds for a couple of minutes, then transfer to a wire rack.

4 Roll out the red ready-to-roll fondant icing and then use a pastry (cookie) cutter to mark lines to look like quilting. Cut out 8 hearts with a cutter about 2.5cm/1in deep. Fold the piece of card into a gutter shape, grease lightly and rest the hearts so that they curve upwards. Set aside to dry.

5 When the cakes are quite cold, cut them in half with a sharp knife and sandwich together with jam (*see* p.153). Mix the icing sugar with lemon juice, 5ml/1 tsp at a time until it is just thin enough to spread over the cakes. Brush loose crumbs off the cakes, then spread the icing over, allowing it to drizzle down the sides, and then position a heart on the top. Dust each cake with a pinch of edible glitter, if you like.

Cook's Tips
Even though the silicone moulds are 'non-stick' it is best to grease them first, either with a little vegetable oil or a spray, and then dust with flour.

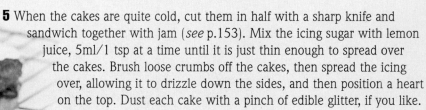

Energy 358kcal/1507kJ; Protein 3g; Carbohydrate 59g, of which sugars 48g; Fat 14g, of which saturates 8g; Cholesterol 90mg; Calcium 65mg; Fibre 1g; Sodium 168mg

PRIVATE DETECTIVE CUPCAKES

Because private detectives always seem to carry a bag of chewy treats in their pocket to keep them going while they keep watch on their suspect, we have made these cupcakes caramel-flavoured with added chunks of gooey toffee in their honour. Our cupcakes are decorated with footprints, a murder scene outline and the essential magnifying glass, but you could also experiment with a torch (flashlight) made out of chocolate, some yellow crime scene tape and even fingerprints drawn with black writing icing.

FOR THE CAKES

115g/4oz/½ cup butter
115g/4oz/scant ¾ cup soft light brown sugar
5ml/1 tsp vanilla extract
2 eggs, lightly beaten
115g/4oz/1 cup self-raising (self-rising) flour, sifted
50g/2oz chewy toffees (caramels), chopped
15–30ml/1–2 tbsp milk

▶▶ **MAKES 12 CUPCAKES**

FOR THE DECORATION

25g/1oz ready-to-roll fondant icing, white
75g/3oz ready-to-roll fondant icing, black
115g/4oz/1 cup icing (confectioners') sugar
½ egg white (about 17g/½oz/generous 1 tbsp)
2.5ml/½ tsp glycerine
2.5ml/½ tsp lemon juice (optional)
5–7.5 ml/1–1½ tsp water
gel or paste food colouring, yellow
writing icing, black

1 Preheat the oven to 180°C/350°F/Gas 4. Line a muffin tin (pan) with cupcake cases.

2 Cream the butter for a few minutes until soft and pale. Add the sugar and continue to beat until the mixture is pale and fluffy. Add the vanilla extract to the lightly beaten eggs and then gradually add to the butter and sugar mixture, beating well between each addition. Add a teaspoon of flour with the last two additions so that the mixture does not curdle. Fold in the sifted flour and the chopped toffees, and then add the milk, a little at a time, until the mixture drops slowly off the spoon.

3 Divide the mixture between the cupcake cases. Bake for 20–25 minutes until risen, lightly browned and bouncy to the touch. Allow the cakes to cool in the tin for a few minutes, then transfer to a wire rack to cool.

4 For the decoration, roll out the white ready-to-roll fondant icing and cut out four circles about 1cm/½in across for the magnifying glasses. Roll out thin strips of black icing and wrap round the edge of the white discs and join together to form a handle (*see* p.154). Set aside to dry. Roll out the remaining black icing and cut out four pairs of footprints. We find it easiest to do this by cutting pairs of rectangles and squares and shaping to form the heel and toe part of the footprint. Set aside to dry.

5 Sift the icing sugar and set aside. Beat the egg white until frothy and then gradually add the sugar, beating until the mixture is thick and glossy. Add the glycerine and lemon juice (if used), and continue beating until the mixture is thick and very white and forms pointy peaks when you lift the whisk. This will take at least 5 minutes with an electric whisk.

6 Stir 5ml/1 tsp water into the icing and test the texture by drawing a knife through the icing and then counting how long the mark takes to fill in. Add a little more water if necessary until you reach the point where the mark fills in after a steady count of 15. Colour the icing bright yellow with food colouring and ice the cupcakes.

7 Arrange footprints on four cakes. Do not forget to put one print slightly in front of the other. Top four cakes with magnifying glasses, and then draw a murder scene cut-out on the remaining cakes with black writing icing.

Energy 238kcal/100kJ; Protein 3g; Carbohydrate 37g, of which sugars 29g; Fat 10g, of which saturates 6g; Cholesterol 61mg; Calcium 52mg; Fibre 0g; Sodium 131mg

SPACE EXPLORER CUPCAKES

Stars and planets glitter and popping candy crackles with these cosmic cakes. Popping candy is carbonated sugar crystals. Sprinkle it on at the last moment because it starts to pop when it touches anything moist.

Popping candy crackles on these cosmic cakes for young astronauts.

FOR THE CAKES

115g/4oz/½ cup butter
115g/4oz/generous ½ cup caster (superfine) sugar
2 eggs, lightly beaten
115g/4oz/1 cup self-raising (self-rising) flour, sifted
75g/3oz milk chocolate chips
15–30ml/1–2 tbsp milk

FOR THE DECORATION

150g/5oz/10tbsp butter, softened
300g/11oz/2½ cups icing (confectioners') sugar, sifted
7.5ml/1½ tsp vanilla extract
10–15ml/2–3 tsp milk
gel or paste food colouring, dark blue
12 lollipops or sherbet flying saucers
edible silver or gold stars
edible glitter
10g/¼oz popping candy

➡➡ MAKES 12 CUPCAKES

1 Preheat the oven to 180°C/350°F/Gas 4. Line a muffin tin (pan) with cupcake cases.

2 Cream the butter for a few minutes until soft and pale. Add the sugar and continue to beat until the mixture is pale and fluffy.

3 Gradually add the eggs, beating well between each addition. Add a teaspoonful of flour with the last two additions so that the mixture does not curdle.

4 Fold in the sifted flour and the chocolate chips (*see* p.154), then add the milk, a little at a time, until the mixture drops slowly off the spoon.

5 Divide the mixture between the cupcake cases. Bake for 20–25 minutes until risen, lightly browned and bouncy to the touch. Allow the cakes to cool in the tin for a few minutes, then transfer to a wire rack to cool completely.

6 For the decoration, cream the butter until soft and pale. Gradually add the sifted icing sugar, beating well between each addition. Beat in the vanilla extract and then add the milk to make the icing just soft enough to pipe.

7 Colour the icing dark blue with food colouring. Pipe a shallow mound of buttercream on each cupcake with a large star nozzle. Stick a lollipop or flying saucer on each cupcake and then decorate with edible stars and glitter. Just before serving, dust with popping candy.

Energy 398kcal/1669kJ; Protein 3g; Carbohydrate 51g, of which sugars 44g; Fat 22g, of which saturates 13g; Cholesterol 88mg; Calcium 63mg; Fibre 0g; Sodium 194mg

FUN AND
Games

Ballet shoes make perfect cupcakes for a little girl.

Ice cream cones instead of cupcake cases.

A little bit of gold at the end of the rainbow.

BALLET SHOES CUPCAKES

Delicate pale pink glacé icing and ballet shoes make perfect cupcakes for a little girl. Rose water, usually found on the shelf with other baking ingredients, gives a wonderful flavour to the cakes and icing, but vanilla or lemon can be used if you prefer. Little sugar flowers are a pretty finishing touch.

FOR THE CAKES
115g/4oz/½ cup butter
115g/4oz/generous ½ cup caster (superfine) sugar
2.5–5ml/½–1 tsp rose water
2 eggs, lightly beaten
115g/4oz/1 cup self-raising (self-rising) flour, sifted
15–30ml/1–2 tbsp milk

▶▶ **MAKES 12 CUPCAKES**

FOR THE DECORATION
250g/9oz ready-to-roll fondant icing, white
gel or paste food colouring, pink
150g/5oz/1¼ cups icing (confectioners') sugar, sifted
30–40ml/2–2½ tbsp water
2–3 drops rose water
mini pink or white sugar flowers, or edible pearls
edible glitter

Cook's Tips
Rose water is surprisingly strongly flavoured, so add it cautiously to the icing.

1 Preheat the oven to 180°C/350°F/Gas 4. Line a muffin tin (pan) with cupcake cases.

2 Cream the butter for a few minutes until soft and pale. Add the sugar and continue to beat until the mixture is pale and fluffy.

3 Add the rose water to the lightly beaten eggs and then gradually add to the butter and sugar mixture, beating well between each addition. Add a teaspoonful of flour with the last two additions of egg, so that the mixture does not curdle.

4 Fold in the sifted flour and then the milk, a little at a time, until the mixture drops slowly off the spoon.

5 Divide the mixture between the cupcake cases. Bake for 20–25 minutes until risen, lightly browned and bouncy to the touch. Allow to cool in the tin for a few minutes, then transfer to a wire rack to cool completely.

6 For the decoration, reserve a golf-ball-sized piece of white icing. Colour the rest of the ready-to-roll fondant icing pale pink. Reserve an additional golf-ball-sized portion of the pink icing. Shape 24 ballet shoes with insoles cut out of the reserved white icing (*see* p.154). Arrange the shoes in pairs and set aside to dry.

7 Mix the icing sugar with water, 5ml/1 tsp at a time, until just thin enough to spread on the cupcake. Be cautious as the icing starts to reach the right consistency. Stir in the rose water.

8 Arrange a pair of ballet shoes on each of the cakes and decorate with sugar flowers or pearls and glitter. Roll out the reserved pink icing. Cut thin strips for ribbons and stick to the ballet shoes.

Energy 277kcal/1168kJ; Protein 2g; Carbohydrate 49g, of which sugars 42g; Fat 9g, of which saturates 5g; Cholesterol 60mg; Calcium 46mg; Fibre 0g; Sodium 116mg

SOCCER FAN CUPCAKES

We have topped chocolate cupcakes with buttercream grass, and footballs and team shirts made with ready-to-roll fondant icing. Needless to say, you should make the shirts in appropriate team colours! Making the footballs is a little fiddly, but the key is to remember that the black panels are five-sided pentagons, and the white panels are six-sided hexagons. It is quite easy to find ready-made football decorations if you prefer.

FOR THE CAKES
90g/3½oz/¾ cup self-raising (self-rising) flour
25g/1oz/¼ cup unsweetened cocoa powder
115g/4oz/½ cup butter
115g/4oz/scant ¾ cup soft light brown sugar
2 eggs, lightly beaten
15–30ml/1–2 tbsp milk

➡ **MAKES 12 CUPCAKES**

FOR THE DECORATION
250g/9oz ready-to-roll fondant icing, white
75g/3oz ready-to-roll fondant icing, red
50g/2oz ready-to-roll fondant icing, black
115g/4oz/½ cup butter, softened
225g/8oz/2 cups icing (confectioners') sugar, sifted
5ml/1 tsp vanilla extract
5–10ml/1–2 tsp milk
gel or paste food colouring, green
food pen, blue

1 Preheat the oven to 180°C/350°F/Gas 4. Line a muffin tin (pan) with cupcake cases. Sift together the flour and the cocoa and set aside.

2 Cream the butter for a few minutes until soft and pale. Add the sugar and continue to beat until the mixture is pale and fluffy. Gradually the lightly beaten eggs to the butter and sugar mixture, beating well between each addition. Add a teaspoonful of flour with each of the last two additions so that the mixture does not curdle. Fold in the sifted flour and cocoa and then add the milk, a little at a time, until the mixture drops slowly off the spoon.

3 Divide the mixture between the cupcake cases. Bake for 20–25 minutes until risen, lightly browned and bouncy to the touch. Allow to cool in the tin for a few minutes, then transfer to a wire rack to cool completely.

4 To make the footballs, take two-thirds of the white ready-to-roll fondant icing, roll six balls about 2.5cm/1in in diameter and cut them in half. Cut 30 pentagons about 5mm/¼in across from the black icing. Moistening the discs, stick black pentagons on each ball. Mark stitching lines with the back of a knife (*see* p.154). Set aside to dry.

5 To make the shirts, cut three shirts from the red icing and three from the white icing. If you would like to make stripes, place a white shirt on a red shirt. Cut vertical strips through both shirts, then separate the strips and reconstruct the shirts in alternating strips. Use a blue food pen to write a number on each shirt. Set aside to dry.

6 Cream the butter until soft and pale. Gradually add the sifted icing sugar, beating well between each addition. Beat in the vanilla extract and then add the milk, a little at a time, until the icing is just soft enough to pipe. Colour it bright green with the food colouring. Pipe grass on the cupcakes with a star piping nozzle. Place one football or shirt in the centre of each cupcake.

Variation – American Footballs: Roll some brown ready-to-roll fondant icing into an elongated ball. Use some white writing icing or a white food pen to draw the stitching across the top of the ball. To create an American football shirt, cut out two shirts in two different colours (here we used blue and white), and cut the shoulder sections away. Separate the pieces and reconstruct the shirts, using one colour for the body and one for the shoulders. Write a number on the front using a black food pen.

Energy 408kcal/1718kJ; Protein 3g; Carbohydrate 64g, of which sugars 58g; Fat 17g, of which saturates 11g; Cholesterol 81mg; Calcium 45mg; Fibre 0g; Sodium 190mg

SUMMER HOLIDAY CUPCAKES

Kites, sandcastles and fishes – holidays on the beach make a bright and cheerful theme for these lemony cakes. You could also try red and yellow beach balls, sailing boats or even lifebelts (preservers). For a small amount of piping it can be more convenient to make a quick piping (pastry) bag with a triangle of baking parchment (*see* page 13).

FOR THE CAKES
115g/4oz/½ cup butter
115g/4oz/generous ½ cup caster (superfine) sugar
2 eggs, lightly beaten
115g/4oz/1 cup self-raising (self-rising) flour, sifted
grated rind of 1 lemon
15–30ml/1–2 tbsp lemon juice

➡➡ MAKES 12 CUPCAKES

FOR THE DECORATION
175g/6oz/1½ cups icing (confectioners') sugar
¾ egg white (about 25g/1oz/1½ tbsp)
5ml/1 tsp glycerine
5ml/1 tsp lemon juice (optional)
5–10ml/1–2 tsp water
gel or paste food colouring, blue, yellow, red
175g/6oz ready-to-roll fondant icing, white

1 Preheat the oven to 180°C/350°F/Gas 4. Line a muffin tin (pan) with cupcake cases.

2 Cream the butter for a few minutes until soft and pale. Add the sugar and continue to beat until the mixture is pale and fluffy. Add the vanilla extract to the lightly beaten eggs and then gradually add to the butter and sugar mixture, beating well between each addition. Add a teaspoonful of flour with the last two additions, so that the mixture does not curdle. Fold in the sifted flour and the grated rind, then add the lemon juice, a little at a time, until the mixture drops slowly off the spoon.

3 Divide the mixture between the cupcake cases. Bake for 20–25 minutes until risen, lightly browned and bouncy to the touch. Allow to cool in the tin for a few minutes, then transfer to a wire rack to cool completely.

4 For the decoration, sift the icing sugar and set aside. Beat the egg white until frothy and then gradually add the sugar, beating until the mixture is thick and glossy. Add the glycerine and lemon juice (if used), and continue beating until the mixture is thick and very white and forms pointy peaks when you lift the whisk. This will take at least 5 minutes with an electric whisk.

5 Reserve about one-third of the icing and cover. Stir 5ml/1 tsp water into the rest of the icing and test the texture by drawing a knife through the icing and then counting how long the mark takes to fill in. Add a little more water if necessary until the mark fills in after a steady count of 15. Colour the icing blue and spread over the cupcakes (*see* p.154).

6 Colour half the ready-to-roll fondant icing yellow and the other half red. Roll out and cut two kite shapes with each colour, then cut into quarters. Cut 12 little bows. Reserve 15ml/1 tbsp royal icing. Colour the remaing royal icing yellow and place in a piping (pastry) bag with a fine round piping nozzle. Re-assemble the kites with alternating colours on the cupcakes, pipe a kite tail and add three bows to each tail.

7 Cut out four sandcastles with yellow icing and four little red flags and four doors. Position the sandcastles on the cupcakes, stick on the doors, pipe whie sticks for the flags and position the flags. Cut four fish from the red icing and pipe yellow scales and eyes on the fish and circular air bubbles on the blue background.

Energy 264kcal/1112kJ; Protein 3g; Carbohydrate 46g, of which sugars 39g; Fat 9g, of which saturates 5g; Cholesterol 60mg; Calcium 44mg; Fibre 0g; Sodium 117mg

DESERT ISLAND CUPCAKES

Pineapple-, banana- and orange-flavoured cupcakes.

FOR THE CAKES
115g/4oz/1 cup plain (all-purpose) flour
115g/4oz/generous ½ cup caster (superfine) sugar
2.5ml/½ tsp bicarbonate of soda (baking soda)
2 eggs, lightly beaten
105ml/7 tbsp sunflower oil
1 ripe banana, mashed
75g/3oz canned pineapple, mashed
grated rind of 1 orange

➤ MAKES 12 CAKES

FOR THE DECORATION
40g/1½oz/3 tbsp butter, softened
115g/4oz/½ cup cream cheese, cold
250g/9oz/2¼ cups icing (confectioners') sugar, sifted
gel or paste food colouring, blue, yellow, black
150g/5oz ready-to-roll fondant icing, white
writing icing, white, green
a few little sugar flowers
6 mini paper parasols

These moist pineapple-, banana- and orange-flavoured cupcakes are a variation of the American classic 'hummingbird' cake and make a deliciously tropical base for desert island cupcakes. We have had fun with islands and sharks – you could also make boats with flag sails. Little paper parasols, sold to decorate cocktail drinks, are usually quite easy to find.

1 Preheat the oven to 180°C/350°F/Gas 4. Line a muffin tin (pan) with cupcake cases.

2 Sift the flour into a large bowl with the sugar and bicarbonate of soda. Add the eggs, oil, banana, pineapple and orange rind (*see* p.155) and stir together until well mixed.

3 Divide the mixture between the cupcake cases. Bake for 20–25 minutes until risen, lightly browned and bouncy to the touch. Allow to cool in the tin for a few minutes, then transfer to a wire rack to cool completely.

4 For the decoration, cream the butter for a few minutes until soft and pale. Drain the cream cheese and beat together with the butter until combined. Do not overbeat. Add half the sifted icing sugar and beat until combined, then beat in the remaining sugar. Colour blue with the food colouring and chill until ready to use.

5 Colour half the ready-to-roll fondant icing yellow and shape six desert islands, as shaped blobs or as layers of cut shapes. Colour the remaining half grey and shape six large shark fins and six small fins. Set aside to dry for a few minutes.

6 Swirl blue icing on the cupcakes to give the effect of a rough sea. Position the islands and small shark fins on six cakes and the large shark fins on the remaining cakes. Pipe wave tops with the white writing icing and leaves on the islands with the green writing icing. Position sugar flowers and a parasol on each of the desert islands.

Energy 363kcal/1526kJ; Protein 3g; Carbohydrate 53g, of which sugars 45g; Fat 17g, of which saturates 6g; Cholesterol 56mg; Calcium 53mg; Fibre 1g; Sodium 150mg

WHITE CHOCOLATE AND RASPBERRY CONES

Flat-bottomed ice cream cones make a fun alternative to cupcake cases for a party. It is simple to make the fresh raspberry purée for the buttercream, but you can use frozen raspberries or a ready-made lightly sweetened raspberry sauce instead.

FOR THE CAKES
12 flat-bottomed ice cream cones
115g/4oz/½ cup butter
115g/4oz/generous ½ cup caster (superfine) sugar
5ml/1 tsp vanilla extract
2 eggs, lightly beaten
115g/4oz/1 cup self-raising (self-rising) flour, sifted
75g/3oz white chocolate chips
15–30ml/1–2 tbsp milk

FOR THE DECORATION
200g/7oz raspberries
5ml/1 tsp lemon juice
175g/6oz/¾ cup butter
350g/12oz/3 cups icing (confectioners') sugar, sifted
sugar sprinkles or freeze-dried raspberries

⇒ MAKES 12 CUPCAKES

Variations
Flavour the cake mixture with a few drops of peppermint extract and use milk chocolate chips. Flavour the buttercream with peppermint extract and decorate with chocolate strands.

1 Preheat the oven to 180°C/350°F/Gas 4. Stand the ice cream cones in a muffin tin (pan).

2 Cream the butter for a few minutes until soft and pale. Add the sugar and continue to beat until the mixture is pale and fluffy.

3 Add the vanilla extract to the lightly beaten eggs and then gradually add to the butter and sugar mixture, beating well between each addition. Add a teaspoonful of flour with the last two additions, so that the mixture does not curdle. Fold in the sifted flour and the chocolate chips, then the milk, a little at a time, until the mixture drops slowly off the spoon.

4 Divide the mixture between the ice cream cones (*see* p.155). Bake for 20–25 minutes until risen, lightly browned and bouncy to the touch. Allow to cool in the tin for a few minutes, then transfer to a wire rack to cool completely.

5 Reserve 12 raspberries for decoration. Place the remaining raspberries in a small pan with the lemon juice and heat gently until the juices run and the raspberries have softened. Press the raspberries through a sieve (strainer) to remove the seeds, and then return the purée to the pan. Simmer gently for 5–6 minutes to thicken and reduce by about a third. Stir occasionally so that the purée does not burn. Turn the purée into a bowl to cool completely – you should have about 45–60ml/3–4 tbsp.

6 Cream the butter until soft and pale. Gradually add the sifted icing sugar, beating well between each addition. Beat in the cooled raspberry purée 15ml/1 tbsp at a time.

7 Pipe swirls of icing on the cones with a large star piping nozzle. Top each cone with one of the reserved raspberries and sprinkle with sugar sprinkles or pieces of freeze-dried raspberry.

We have hidden white chocolate chip cupcakes inside these cones.

Energy 433kcal/1818kJ; Protein 4g; Carbohydrate 56g, of which sugars 45g;
Fat 23g, of which saturates 14g; Cholesterol 91mg; Calcium 77mg; Fibre 2g; Sodium 212mg

MIX AND MATCH CUPCAKES

We've made an edible version of the traditional mix-and-match game with these orange-flavoured cupcakes. There are four heads, four bodies and four sets of legs that you can arrange in whatever order you choose before eating them. Try portraits of members of the family, or go wild and create some fantasy outfits or mix-and-match animal heads and bodies, or even robots and monsters.

FOR THE CAKES
115g/4oz/½ cup butter
115g/4oz/generous ½ cup caster (superfine) sugar
2 eggs, lightly beaten
115g/4oz/1 cup self-raising (self-rising) flour, sifted
grated rind of 1 orange
15–30ml/1–2 tbsp orange juice

▶▶ MAKES 12 CUPCAKES

FOR THE DECORATION
115g/4oz/1 cup icing (confectioners') sugar
½ egg white (about 17g/½oz/generous 1 tbsp)
2.5ml/½ tsp glycerine
5ml/1 tsp orange juice (optional)
5–10ml/1–2 tsp water
range of gel or paste food colourings including green
175g/6oz ready-to-roll fondant icing, white
flat sprinkles (optional)
writing icing, red, blue and black

1 Preheat the oven to 180°C/350°F/Gas 4. Line a muffin tin (pan) with cupcake cases.

2 Cream the butter for a few minutes until soft and pale. Add the sugar and continue to beat until the mixture is pale and fluffy. Gradually add the lightly beaten eggs to the butter and sugar mixture, beating well between each addition. Add a teaspoonful of flour with each of the last two additions, so that the mixture does not curdle. Fold in the sifted flour and the grated rind, then the juice, a little at a time, until the mixture drops slowly off the spoon.

3 Divide the mixture between the cupcake cases. Bake for 20–25 minutes until risen, lightly browned and bouncy to the touch. Allow to cool in the tin for a few minutes, then transfer to a wire rack to cool completely.

4 For the decoration, sift the icing sugar and set aside. Beat the egg white until frothy and then gradually add the sugar, beating until the mixture is thick and glossy. Add the glycerine and juice (if used), and continue beating until the mixture is thick and very white and forms pointy peaks when you lift the whisk. This will take at least 5 minutes with an electric whisk.

5 Stir 5ml/1 tsp water into the rest of the icing and test the texture by drawing a knife through the icing and then counting how long the mark takes to fill in. Add a little more water if necessary until you reach the point where the mark fills in after a steady count of 15. Colour the icing green and spread it on the cupcakes.

6 Take roughly one third of the ready-to-roll fondant icing and colour it in skin tones. Reserve a quarter of this icing to make arms and necks then roll out and shape four heads.

7 Reserve about a quarter of the remaining white icing (this will be used for shoes) and divide the rest of the icing into four. Colour each one a different colour. Cut a T-shirt and a pair of trousers out of two of the colours and a T-shirt and a skirt out of the remaining colours (*see* p.155). You can decorate the clothes, if you wish, by pressing flat sprinkles into the icing, by making contrasting icing stripes or hems, or indenting a pattern.

8 Assemble four heads, four body sections and four leg sections, making legs, shoes and hair out of the reserved icing, coloured as appropriate. Pipe eyes and mouths with writing icing and mark noses with a cocktail stick (toothpick).

Energy 244kcal/1030kJ; Protein 2g; Carbohydrate 41g, of which sugars 33g; Fat 9g, of which saturates 5g; Cholesterol 60mg; Calcium 44mg; Fibre 0g; Sodium 116mg

MINI MACARON LOLLIPOPS

Little French macarons on lollipop sticks or nestled in petit four cases make wonderful child-sized treats in bright colours. They are not difficult to make as long as you measure the ingredients and follow the instructions carefully. If you want to make more than one colour, it is better to make two separate batches of mixture.

FOR THE MACARONS
90g/3½oz ground almonds
115g/4oz icing (confectioners') sugar
75g/3oz egg white (roughly two medium eggs)
50g/2oz caster (superfine) sugar
gel or paste food colouring, green
sugar sprinkles in contrasting colours (optional)

➡️ **MAKES ABOUT 30 MACARONS**

FOR THE BUTTERCREAM
50g/2oz/¼ cup butter, softened
115g/4oz/1 cup icing (confectioners')
  sugar, sifted
5–10ml/1–2 tsp lemon juice
gel or paste food colouring, yellow
about 30 short lollipop or
  cake-pop sticks
about 30 petit four cases to serve

Cook's Tips
Add sprinkles in contrasting colours after piping the macarons so that they stick to the surface. Try other colours for the macarons and filling.

1 Line two baking sheets with baking parchment.

2 Put the ground almonds and the icing sugar in a food processor and process for 2–3 minutes until the mixture is very fine. Do not over-process. Sift the sugar and almond mixture into a bowl and set aside. Discard any bits of almond left in the sieve (strainer) – do not force them through.

3 Place the egg whites in a large, grease-free bowl and whisk until they form soft peaks. Whisk in half the caster sugar, then whisk in the rest. Continue whisking until the mixture is thick and shiny. Colour the mixture bright green with food colouring.

4 Fold half the sifted almonds and sugar into the eggs. Then fold in the other half. Keep on folding for 1–2 minutes until the mixture runs off the spoon in a ribbon when you hold it up. Stop folding now.

5 Put the mixture in a piping (pastry) bag with a plain round nozzle and pipe 60–70 small circles about 1½–2cm/½–¾in across. Sprinkle a few decorations on the macarons, if you like (*see* p.155).

6 Leave the trays for 30 minutes, so that a thin skin forms on top of the macarons. This will produce the effect of a bubbly 'foot' around the base of the macarons when they are cooked. Preheat the oven to 160°C/325°F/Gas 3.

7 Bake the macarons for 10–12 minutes until the macarons are risen and smooth with a 'foot' and just starting to colour. Allow to cool completely on the tray, then remove them from the paper with a sharp knife.

8 Cream the butter until soft and pale. Gradually add the sifted icing sugar, beating well between each addition. Beat in enough of the juice to make the icing just soft enough to pipe. Colour the icing yellow with the food colouring.

9 Match up the shells for size and shape. Pipe or spread buttercream on the flat side of half the macaron shells. Press a lollipop stick into the filling and sandwich a second half on top. Chill until set or overnight. Serve in petit four cases.

Energy 68kcal/288kJ; Protein 1g; Carbohydrate 10g, of which sugars 10g; Fat 3g, of which saturates 1g; Cholesterol 4mg; Calcium 8mg; Fibre 0g; Sodium 16mg

Mini macarons make
wonderful child-sized treats …

RAINBOW MAGIC
CUPCAKES

Cook's Tips

It is easiest to divide mixture into portions by weight. Each portion of cake mixture weighs about 115g/4oz and each portion of icing weighs about 130g/4½oz.

Spoon alternate colours into the piping bag.

FOR THE CAKES

115g/4oz/½ cup butter
115g/4oz/generous ½ cup caster (superfine) sugar
5ml/1 tsp vanilla extract
2 eggs, lightly beaten
115g/4oz/1 cup self-raising (self-rising) flour, sifted
15–30ml/1–2 tbsp milk
gel or paste food colouring, red, blue, yellow, green

➡ MAKES 12 CUPCAKES

FOR THE DECORATION

175g/6oz/¾ cup butter
350g/12oz/3 cups icing (confectioners') sugar, sifted
2.5ml/½ tsp vanilla extract
10–15ml/2–3 tsp milk
gel or paste food colouring, red, blue, yellow, green
edible gold glitter (optional)

We have topped multi-coloured cakes with swirls of multi-coloured icing and a dusting of edible glitter – a little bit of gold at the end of the rainbow. Getting the rainbow piping effect right can be a bit fiddly, and we have allowed a little more buttercream than usual given that some will inevitably get wasted along the way, but the effect is well worth the effort.

1 Preheat the oven to 180°C/350°F/Gas 4. Line a muffin tin (pan) with cupcake cases.

2 Cream the butter for a few minutes until soft and pale. Add the sugar and continue to beat until the mixture is pale and fluffy. Add the vanilla extract to the lightly beaten eggs and then gradually add to the butter and sugar mixture, beating well between each addition. Add a teaspoonful of flour with the last two additions, so that the mixture does not curdle. Fold in the sifted flour and then add the milk, a little at a time, until the mixture drops slowly off the spoon. Divide the mixture into four and colour one portion red, one blue, one yellow and one green.

3 Scraping every last bit of mixture out of the bowls, put a spoonful of each colour into each cupcake case. Swirl lightly together with a skewer or cocktail stick (toothpick) (*see* p.155). Bake for 20–25 minutes until risen, lightly browned and bouncy to the touch. Allow to cool in the tin for a few minutes, then transfer to a wire rack to cool completely.

4 For the decoration, cream the butter until soft and pale. Gradually add the sifted icing sugar, beating well between each addition. Beat in the vanilla extract and then enough of the milk to make the icing just soft enough to pipe.

5 Divide the icing into four portions and colour them red, blue, yellow and green. Fit a piping (pastry) bag with a large star piping nozzle, and then place it in a glass or mug with the top of the bag rolled down. Spoon alternating colours into the piping bag, a spoonful at a time. Pipe swirls of icing on to the cupcakes, squeezing the bag gently so that the colours stay as separate as possible. Dust the cupcakes with edible glitter, if you like.

Energy 379kcal/1590kJ; Protein 2g; Carbohydrate 48g, of which sugars 41g; Fat 21g of which saturates 13g;
Cholesterol 91mg; Calcium 48mg; Fibre 0g; Sodium 200mg

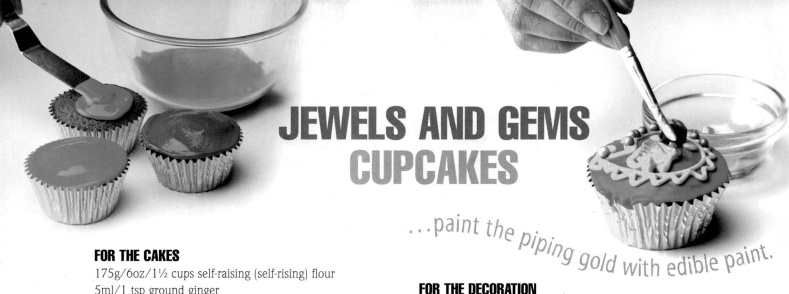

JEWELS AND GEMS CUPCAKES

...paint the piping gold with edible paint.

FOR THE CAKES

175g/6oz/1½ cups self-raising (self-rising) flour
5ml/1 tsp ground ginger
2.5ml/½ tsp bicarbonate of soda (baking soda)
90g/3½oz/7 tbsp butter
90g/3½oz/7 tbsp soft light brown sugar
90g/3½oz/¼ cup golden (light corn) syrup
100ml/3½fl oz/scant ½ cup milk
1 egg, lightly beaten

➡ **MAKES 12 CAKES**

FOR THE DECORATION

225g/8oz/2 cups icing (confectioners') sugar
1 egg white
10ml/2 tsp glycerine
10ml/2 tsp lemon juice (optional)
10–15ml/2–3 tsp water
gel or paste food colouring, pink, green, turquoise, yellow
edible gems or boiled sweets (candies), edible pearls, dragées
edible gold paint

Delicious cakes lightly spiced with ginger are the base for these pretty cupcakes with Indian-inspired designs. We love ginger, but it is a love-or-hate flavour for children, and of course you can substitute a different-flavoured cake if your child is in the hate camp. Edible gold paint is available online or from specialist cake suppliers.

1 Preheat the oven to 160°C/325°F/Gas 3 (this is slightly lower than the temperature we usually use). Line a muffin tin (pan) with cupcake cases. Sift together the flour, ginger and bicarbonate of soda.

2 Put the butter, sugar and syrup in a medium pan and stir over low heat until the ingredients are melted together.

3 Remove from the heat and stir in first the milk and then the egg. Add the sifted flour mixture and stir until smooth.

4 Divide the mixture between the cupcake cases. Bake for 20–25 minutes until risen, lightly browned and bouncy to the touch. Allow to cool in the tin for a few minutes, then transfer to a wire rack to cool completely.

5 For the decoration, sift the icing sugar and set aside. Beat the egg white until frothy and then gradually add the sugar, beating until the mixture is thick and glossy. Add the glycerine and lemon juice (if used), and continue beating until the mixture is thick and very white and forms pointy peaks when you lift the whisk. This will take at least 5 minutes with an electric whisk.

6 Reserve about a third of the icing and cover. Stir 5ml/1 tsp water into the remaining icing and test the texture by drawing a knife through the icing and then counting how long the mark takes to fill in. Add a little more water if necessary until you reach the point where the mark fills in after a steady count of 15.

7 Divide the icing into three and colour one portion deep pink, one portion bright green and one portion deep turquoise blue and cover four cupcakes with each colour (*see* p.156). Set aside to dry.

8 Colour the reserved icing yellow and, using a fine plain piping nozzle, pipe paisley patterns on each cupcake. Arrange edible gems, pearls or dragées on the lines. Set aside to dry. Once the lines of piping are completely dry, paint them gold with the edible paint.

Energy 239kcal/1011kJ; Protein 3g; Carbohydrate 45g, of which sugars 34g; Fat 7g, of which saturates 4g; Cholesterol 36mg; Calcium 71mg; Fibre 1g; Sodium 184mg

TASTY
and
Delicious

Fresh blueberries make juicy cupcakes.

Mint chocolate
chip is always a
favourite.

Add lemon rind and berries ...

PERFECT PURPLE CUPCAKES

Fresh blueberries make these cupcakes deliciously juicy. We have topped them with pale purple cream cheese frosting and more fresh blueberries, but a simple glacé icing made with lemon juice would also work well. We were thrilled to find silicone teacup-style cases with handles!

... and decorate with blueberries and sugar sprinkles.

FOR THE CAKES
115g/4oz/½ cup butter
115g/4oz/generous ½ cup caster (superfine) sugar
2 eggs, lightly beaten
115g/4oz/1 cup self-raising (self-rising) flour, sifted
grated rind of 1 lemon
200g/7oz/1⅓ cup blueberries, washed and dried
15–30ml/1–2 tbsp lemon juice

FOR THE DECORATION
40g/1½oz/3 tbsp butter, softened
115g/4oz/½ cup cream cheese, cold
250g/9oz/2¼ cups icing (confectioners') sugar, sifted
gel or paste food colouring, purple
purple sugar sprinkles

➡➡ **MAKES 12 CUPCAKES**

1 Preheat the oven to 180°C/350°F/Gas 4. Line a muffin tin (pan) with cupcake cases. Set aside about 60 blueberries to decorate the cupcakes.

2 Cream the butter for a few minutes until soft and pale. Add the sugar and continue to beat until the mixture is pale and fluffy.

3 Gradually add the lightly beaten eggs to the butter and sugar mixture, beating well between each addition. Add a teaspoonful of flour with each of the last two additions, so that the mixture does not curdle.

4 Fold in the sifted flour, the grated rind and the berries (*see* p.156), then add the juice, a little at a time, until the mixture drops slowly off the spoon.

5 Divide the mixture between the cupcake cases. Bake for 20–25 minutes until risen, lightly browned and bouncy to the touch. Allow to cool in the tin for a few minutes, then transfer to a wire rack to cool completely.

6 For the decoration, cream the butter for a few minutes until soft and pale. Drain the cream cheese and beat together with the butter until combined. Do not overbeat. Add half the sifted icing sugar and beat until combined, then beat in the remaining sugar. Colour pale purple with a drop of food colouring.

7 Top each cupcake with a swirl of icing, then decorate with the reserved blueberries and some sugar sprinkles.

Energy 313kcal/1314kJ; Protein 3g; Carbohydrate 42g, of which sugars 32g; Fat 16g, of which saturates 10g; Cholesterol 76mg; Calcium 53mg; Fibre 0g; Sodium 160mg

There is a surprise hidden in the middle.

CHOCOLATE EXPLOSION CUPCAKES

FOR THE CAKES

90g/3½oz/¾ cup self-raising (self-rising) flour
25g/1oz/¼ cup unsweetened cocoa powder
115g/4oz/½ cup butter
115g/4oz/scant ¾ cup soft light brown sugar
2 eggs, lightly beaten
15–30ml/1–2 tbsp milk
6 large or 12 small squares of milk chocolate (about 40g/1½oz in total)

FOR THE DECORATION

50g/2oz plain (semisweet) chocolate
115g/4oz/½ cup butter, softened
225g/8oz/2 cups icing (confectioners') sugar, sifted
5–10ml/1–2 tsp milk
chocolates and chocolate sprinkles

▶▶ MAKES 12 CUPCAKES

1 Preheat the oven to 180°C/350°F/Gas 4. Line a muffin tin (pan) with cupcake cases.

2 Sift together the flour and the cocoa and set aside. Cream the butter for a few minutes until soft and pale. Add the sugar and continue to beat until the mixture is pale and fluffy.

3 Gradually add the lightly beaten eggs to the butter and sugar mixture, beating well between each addition. Add a teaspoonful of flour with each of the last two additions, so that the mixture does not curdle. Fold in the sifted flour and cocoa and then the milk, a little at a time, until the mixture drops slowly off the spoon.

4 If necessary, cut large squares of milk chocolate in half. Put a teaspoonful of mixture in each cupcake case and place a piece of chocolate on top (*see* p.156). Divide the rest of the mixture between the cases. Bake for 20–25 minutes until risen, lightly browned and bouncy to the touch. Take the cakes out of the oven, leave for a few minutes in the tin and then remove and cool on a rack.

5 Melt the decoration chocolate in a microwave or in a bowl over a pan of gently simmering water. Set aside to cool.

6 Cream the butter until soft and pale. Gradually add the sifted icing sugar, beating well between each addition. Beat in the cooled, melted chocolate and then add the milk, a little at a time, if necessary, to make the icing just soft enough to pipe. Pipe a shallow swirl of icing on each cake, and then decorate with a mixture of chocolates.

For children who *really, really* like chocolate, there is a surprise hidden in the middle of these very chocolatey cakes in the form of a square of milk chocolate. Chocolate-coated caramels are also delicious. Have fun with a variety of chocolate treats for the decoration.

Energy 341kcal/1427kJ; Protein 3g; Carbohydrate 41g, of which sugars 34g; Fat 20g, of which saturates 12g; Cholesterol 82mg; Calcium 57mg; Fibre 0g; Sodium 87mg

HONEYBEE CUPCAKES

FOR THE CAKES

115g/4oz/½ cup butter
50g/2oz/generous ¼ cup caster (superfine) sugar
65g/2½oz/¼ cup honey
2 eggs, lightly beaten
115g/4oz/1 cup self-raising (self-rising) flour, sifted
15–30ml/1–2 tbsp milk

FOR THE DECORATION

115g/4oz ready-to-roll fondant icing, white
gel or paste food colouring, yellow, black
20–30 almond flakes (slices)
black food pen or writing icing
175g/6oz/¾ cup butter
350g/12oz/3 cups icing (confectioners') sugar, sifted
15ml/3 tsp honey
15ml/3 tsp lemon juice
5–10ml/1–2 tsp milk (if required)

➡➡ MAKES 12 CUPCAKES

Honey-flavoured cupcakes are topped with piped honey-and-lemon buttercream beehives. We have had fun making bees from ready-to-roll fondant icing, but it is possible to find ready-made edible bee decorations if you prefer.

      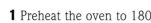

1 Preheat the oven to 180°C/350°F/Gas 4. Line a muffin tin (pan) with cupcake cases.

2 Cream the butter for a few minutes until soft and pale. Add the sugar and honey and continue to beat until the mixture is pale and fluffy.

3 Gradually add the lightly beaten eggs to the butter mixture, beating well between each addition. Add a teaspoonful of flour with the last two additions, so that the mixture does not curdle.

4 Fold in the sifted flour, then add the milk, a little at a time, until the mixture drops slowly off the spoon (*see* p.156).

5 Divide the mixture between the cupcake cases. Bake for 20–25 minutes until risen, lightly browned and bouncy to the touch. Allow to cool in the tin for a few minutes, then transfer to a wire rack to cool completely.

6 Reserve about 25g/1 oz of ready-to-roll fondant icing and cover. Colour the remaining icing yellow. Shape 12 or more bee bodies (they have necks, slightly pointed tails and curved bodies). Colour the reserved icing black. Roll out and cut thin strips of black icing and wrap around the bee bodies for stripes. Fix a pair of almond flakes (or pieces of flake) on each bee as wings, and draw eyes and a mouth on the head with the food pen. Set aside to dry.

7 Cream the butter for a few minutes until soft and pale. Gradually add the sifted icing sugar, beating well between each addition, then add the honey and juice. Beat in the milk if necessary to make the icing just soft enough to pipe.

8 Colour the buttercream pale yellow with food colouring. Pipe a hive-shaped mound of buttercream in the centre of each cupcake with a large plain piping nozzle. Position 1 or 2 bees on each buttercream hive.

Energy 415kcal/1741kJ; Protein 3g; Carbohydrate 56g, of which sugars 49g; Fat 22g, of which saturates 13g; Cholesterol 91mg; Calcium 50mg; Fibre 1g; Sodium 203mg

WHITE CHOCOLATE AND RASPBERRY CAKE POPS

Dip the whole cake pop in the chocolate ...

Have fun dressing up these simple but delicious cake pops. Ribbons or lacy collars made with paper doilies look pretty, and cellophane bags tied with ribbons make the pops easier to transport. The raspberry flavour comes from raspberry buttercream and a sprinkling of pieces of dried raspberry on each pop, but if you can't find dried raspberry they will taste great just sprinkled with coloured sugar crystals.

... and decorate with pieces of dried raspberry.

FOR THE CAKE POPS
65g/2½oz/5 tbsp butter, softened
150g/5oz/1¼ cups icing (confectioners') sugar, sifted
30ml/2 tbsp raspberry jam, sieved (strained)
5–10ml/1–2 tsp lemon juice
375–400g/13–14oz vanilla or lemon sponge cake
 (*see* recipe p.16 or use store-bought)

FOR THE DECORATION
250–300g/7–11oz white chocolate
24 cake pop sticks
pink and white sugar sprinkles
freeze-dried raspberries

➤➤ MAKES 20–24 CAKE POPS

1 Cream the butter for a few minutes until soft and light. Gradually add the icing sugar, beating between each addition. Beat in the raspberry jam and the lemon juice (*see* p.156).

2 Crumble the cake into fine crumbs (this is easiest to do in a food processor), and put the crumbs in a large bowl. Mix in the buttercream, a spoonful at a time. The mixture needs to bind together and be mouldable but not too wet. You may not need to use all the buttercream. Shape the mixture into round balls weighing about 25g/1oz each. Chill the balls for 30 minutes until firm but not completely solid.

3 For the decoration, melt the white chocolate in a microwave or in a bowl set over a pan of gently simmering water. Dip each cake pop stick in the chocolate and then insert it about halfway into a ball. Repeat with the remaining balls and chill until firm, if necessary.

4 If the white chocolate has hardened, heat it again gently until melted. Twirl the whole cake pop in the chocolate, using a spoon if necessary to help with covering the cake. Gently shake off excess chocolate and decorate with sugar sprinkles and pieces of dried raspberry. Stick the pop into a block of polystyrene (Styrofoam) or florists' foam and leave to dry. Continue with the remaining pops in the same way.

Energy 362kcal/1515kJ; Protein 4g; Carbohydrate 44g, of which sugars 37g; Fat 20g, of which saturates 12g; Cholesterol 72mg; Calcium 100mg; Fibre 0g; Sodium 165mg

MARSHMALLOW MINT CHOCOLATE WHOOPIE PIES

FOR THE CAKES
75g/3oz/6 tbsp butter
130g/4½oz/¾ cup soft light brown sugar
5ml/1 tsp vanilla extract
1 egg, lightly beaten
175g/6oz/1½ cups self-raising (self-rising) flour
2.5ml/½ tsp baking powder
25g/1oz/¼ cup unsweetened cocoa powder
120ml/4fl oz/½ cup milk

▶▶ MAKES 16 SMALL WHOOPIE PIES

FOR THE DECORATION
75g/3oz/6 tbsp butter, softened
150g/5oz/1¼ cups icing (confectioners') sugar, sifted
4–5 drops peppermint extract
150g/5oz marshmallow fluff
150g/5oz/1¼ cups icing (confectioners') sugar, sifted
30–40ml/2–2½ tbsp water or lemon juice
gel or paste food colouring, green
edible pearls

1 Preheat the oven to 190°C/375°F/Gas 5. Line two large baking sheets with baking parchment.

2 Cream the butter for a few minutes until soft and pale. Add the sugar and continue to beat until the mixture is pale and fluffy. Add the vanilla extract to the lightly beaten egg and then gradually add to the butter and sugar mixture, beating well between each addition.

3 Sift the flour with the baking powder and cocoa. Stir half the flour into the mixture, then stir in half the milk. Stir in the remaining flour and then the remaining milk until the mixture is well combined, but do not over mix.

4 Using a teaspoon, spoon 16 rounds of mixture on each baking sheet – 32 in total. Use a wetted finger to smooth the tops. Bake for 10–12 minutes until risen, lightly coloured and bouncy to the touch. Leave to cool on the baking sheets for a couple of minutes, then transfer to a wire rack to cool using a palette knife (*see* p.157).

5 For the decoration, cream the butter until soft and pale. Gradually add the sifted icing sugar, beating well between each addition. Beat in the peppermint extract. Fold in the marshmallow fluff until the mixture is smooth.

6 Match up the cakes for size and shape. Pipe the marshmallow filling on the flat side of half the cakes using a large star piping nozzle or spread it on the cakes. Sandwich the cakes together.

7 To make the glacé icing, mix the icing sugar with water or lemon juice just 5ml/1 tsp at a time until thin enough to spread. Be cautious as the icing starts to reach the right consistency. Colour the icing pale green. Spread icing on the filled pies, and top each with a sprinkling of edible pearls.

Mint chocolate chip ice cream is a favourite with many children,
so we have devised a chocolate whoopie pie filled with fluffy mint filling made with an amazing ingredient called marshmallow fluff. This fluffy white substance comes in jars and is used in the traditional whoopie pie filling. It is really delicious, and this mint variation is especially good. It is becoming more widely available in supermarkets.

Energy 254kcal/1070kJ; Protein 2g; Carbohydrate 45g, of which sugars 34g; Fat 9g, of which saturates 5g; Cholesterol 35mg; Calcium 60mg; Fibre 0g; Sodium 142mg

Variations

For a simple lemon drizzle topping, add the zest and juice of 1 lemon to 75g/3oz/ generous ⅓ cup caster (superfine) sugar, then spoon it over the cakes as soon as they come out of the oven.

Little buns filled with raisins are a treat just by themselves, but lemon-flavoured glacé icing makes them even more delicious. We found pretty edible wafer daisies and bright yellow and green coloured sugar sprinkles for decoration, but you could also make your own daisies from ready-to-roll fondant icing.

FOR THE CAKES
115g/4oz/½ cup butter
115g/4oz/generous ½ cup caster (superfine) sugar
2 eggs, lightly beaten
115g/4oz/1 cup self-raising (self-rising) flour, sifted
grated rind of 1 lemon
75g/3oz/½ cup raisins
15–30ml/1–2 tbsp lemon juice

FOR THE DECORATION
150g/5oz/1¼ cups icing (confectioners') sugar, sifted
30–40ml/2–2½ tbsp water or lemon juice
yellow and green sugar sprinkles
12 edible flowers

➤➤ **MAKES 12 CUPCAKES**

1 Preheat the oven to 180°C/350°F/Gas 4. Line a muffin tin (pan) with cupcake cases.

2 Cream the butter for a few minutes until soft and pale. Add the sugar and continue to beat until the mixture is pale and fluffy.

3 Gradually add the lightly beaten eggs to the butter and sugar mixture, beating well between each addition. Add a teaspoonful of flour with each of the last two additions, so that the mixture does not curdle.

4 Fold in the sifted flour, the grated rind and the raisins, then add the juice, a little at a time, until the mixture drops slowly off the spoon.

5 Divide the mixture between the cupcake cases. Bake for 20–25 minutes until risen, lightly browned and bouncy to the touch (*see* p.157). Allow to cool in the tin for a few minutes, then transfer to a wire rack to cool.

6 For the decoration, mix the icing sugar with water or lemon juice 5ml/1 tsp at a time until thin enough to spread on the cupcake. Be cautious as the icing starts to reach the right consistency. Ice the cupcakes and decorate with the sprinkles and flowers.

Energy 222kcal/933kJ; Protein 2g; Carbohydrate 35g, of which sugars 28g; Fat 9g, of which saturates 5g; Cholesterol 60mg; Calcium 45mg; Fibre 1g; Sodium 113mg

STRAWBERRIES AND CREAM CUPCAKES

Everyone loves strawberries in the summer and each of these cupcakes has a strawberry jam surprise at the centre and a topping of lightly sweetened whipped cream and fresh strawberries. You could easily adapt the recipe to use with raspberries or other soft fruit. It is best to add the topping just before serving.

FOR THE CAKES
115g/4oz/½ cup butter
115g/4oz/generous ½ cup caster (superfine) sugar
2.5ml/½ tsp vanilla extract
2 eggs, lightly beaten
115g/4oz/1 cup self-raising (self-rising) flour, sifted
15–30ml/1–2 tbsp milk
about 115g/4oz/⅓ cup strawberry jam

FOR THE DECORATION
175ml/6fl oz/ml/¾ cup double (heavy) cream or whipping cream
10ml/2 tsp caster (superfine) sugar (optional)
6–8 fresh strawberries, washed and dried

▶▶ MAKES 12 CUPCAKES

Variations
If you like your cupcakes moist, you can replace the strawberry jam with about 75–100g/3–3½oz fresh strawberries, chopped and stirred into the cake mixture. Cook for 25–30 minutes.

1 Preheat the oven to 180°C/350°F/Gas 4. Line a muffin tin (pan) with cupcake cases.

2 Cream the butter for a few minutes until soft and pale. Add the sugar and continue to beat until the mixture is pale and fluffy.

3 Mix the vanilla extract with the lightly beaten eggs and then gradually add to the butter and sugar mixture, beating well between each addition. Add a teaspoonful of flour with the last two additions, so that the mixture does not curdle.

4 Fold in the sifted flour and then add the milk, a little at a time, until the mixture drops slowly off the spoon.

5 Put a teaspoonful of mixture in each of the cupcake cases and make a dip in the middle. Put about 2.5ml/½ tsp of strawberry jam in each case (*see* p.157). Bake for 20–25 minutes until risen, lightly browned and bouncy to the touch. Allow to cool in the tin for a few minutes, then transfer to a wire rack to cool completely.

6 Before serving, whip the cream with the sugar (if used) until it stands in soft peaks. Pipe a swirl of cream on the top of each cupcake with a large star piping nozzle. Hull the strawberries. Cut the strawberries into vertical slices and arrange two or three slices on the top of the swirl of cream in a fan shape.

Energy 258kcal/1079kJ; Protein 3g; Carbohydrate 26g, of which sugars 18g; Fat 17g, of which saturates 10g; Cholesterol 80mg; Calcium 53mg; Fibre 1g; Sodium 114mg

COCONUT ICE CUPCAKES

There is something very enticing about coconut ice in pretty clear bags tied with ribbons, and we have been inspired to make a cupcake version of this childhood favourite. Pink and white coconut cakes are topped with a swirl of cream cheese icing and decorated with pale pink coconut.

Sprinkle with pink coconut and a light dust of edible glitter.

FOR THE CAKES
115g/4oz/½ cup butter
115g/4oz/generous ½ cup caster (superfine) sugar
2 eggs, lightly beaten
115g/4oz/1 cup self-raising (self-rising) flour, sifted
50g/2oz/scant ⅔ cup desiccated (dry unsweetened shredded) coconut
30–45ml/2–3 tbsp milk
gel or paste food colouring, pink

FOR THE DECORATION
gel or paste food colouring, pink
50g/2oz/scant ⅔ cup desiccated (dry unsweetened shredded) coconut
40g/1½oz/3 tbsp butter, softened
115g/4oz/½ cup cream cheese, cold
250g/9oz/2¼ cups icing (confectioners') sugar, sifted
edible glitter (optional)

➡➡ MAKES 12 CUPCAKES

1 Preheat the oven to 180°C/350°F/Gas 4. Line a muffin tin (pan) with cupcake cases.

2 Cream the butter for a few minutes until soft and pale. Add the sugar and continue to beat until the mixture is pale and fluffy.

3 Gradually add the eggs, beating well between each addition. Add a teaspoonful of flour with the last two additions, so that the mixture does not curdle.

4 Fold in the sifted flour and the coconut, then add the milk, a little at a time, until the mixture drops slowly off the spoon.

5 Spoon half the mixture into another bowl and colour pink with the food colouring. Divide the pink mixture between the cupcake cases and then add the plain mixture (*see* p.157). Bake for 20–25 minutes until risen, lightly browned and bouncy to the touch. Allow to cool in the tin for a couple of minutes, then transfer to a wire rack to cool completely.

6 For the decoration, put a few drops of pink food colouring in a jam jar with a lid. If you are using stiff paste, add a drop or two or water to liquify the colour. Put the coconut for decoration in the jar, put on the lid and shake hard until the coconut is coloured pink. Spread the coconut out on a plate to dry, if necessary.

7 Cream the butter for a few minutes until soft and pale. Drain the cream cheese and beat together with the butter until combined. Do not overbeat. Add half the sifted icing sugar and beat until combined, then beat in the remaining sugar.

8 Top each cupcake with a swirl of icing, then sprinkle with the pink coconut and a light dust of edible glitter, if used.

Energy 355kcal/1485kJ; Protein 3g; Carbohydrate 40g, of which sugars 33g; Fat 22g, of which saturates 14g; Cholesterol 76mg; Calcium 56mg; Fibre 2g; Sodium 162mg

MAPLE SYRUP CUPCAKES

Maple syrup gives a delicate toffee flavour to cupcakes and buttercream icing, and if your child likes nuts you can use pecans or walnuts in the recipe. We have found some clever maple-leaf cutters and have used them to decorate these cakes with leaves made from ready-to-roll fondant icing but any leaf shapes coloured in orange, yellow and brown would look pretty. Simple halved or chopped nuts make a quick alternative.

FOR THE CAKES
115g/4oz/½ cup butter
115g/4oz/scant ½ cup soft light brown sugar
2 eggs, lightly beaten
115g/4oz/1 cup self-raising (self-rising) flour, sifted
45ml/3 tbsp maple syrup
50g/2oz chopped pecans or walnuts
15–30ml/1–2 tbsp milk

FOR THE DECORATION
150g/5oz ready-to-roll fondant icing
gel or paste food colouring, yellow, brown
115g/4oz/½ cup butter, softened
225g/8oz/2 cups icing (confectioners') sugar, sifted
20ml/4 tsp maple syrup
5–10ml/1–2 tsp milk

➤➤ **MAKES 12 CUPCAKES**

1 Preheat the oven to 180°C/350°F/Gas 4. Line a muffin tin (pan) with cupcake cases.

2 Cream the butter for a few minutes until soft and pale. Add the sugar and continue to beat until the mixture is pale and fluffy.

3 Gradually add the lightly beaten eggs to the butter mixture, beating well between each addition. Add a teaspoonful of flour with the last two additions, so that the mixture does not curdle. Beat in the syrup.

4 Fold in the sifted flour and the nuts, and then the milk, a little at a time, if necessary, until the mixture drops slowly off the spoon (*see* p.157).

5 Divide the mixture between the cupcake cases. Bake for 20–25 minutes until risen, lightly browned and bouncy to the touch. Allow to cool in the tin for a few minutes, then transfer to a wire rack to cool completely

6 For the decoration, colour half the ready-to-roll fondant icing yellow, and the other half brown. Roll out and cut leaves in both colours – at least 24 in total. Set aside to dry.

7 Cream the butter until soft and pale. Gradually add the sifted icing sugar, beating well between each addition. Beat in the maple syrup and then add the milk, if necessary, to make the icing just soft enough to pipe.

8 Pipe a shallow mound of icing on each of the cupcakes with a large star piping nozzle or swirl with a knife. Arrange a pair of leaves on each cupcake.

Energy 384kcal/1609kJ; Protein 3g; Carbohydrate 52g, of which sugars 44g; Fat 20g, of which saturates 11g; Cholesterol 81mg; Calcium 60mg; Fibre 1g; Sodium 175mg

RECIPES
Step-by-Step

Puppies and Kittens   p.24

Knead food colouring into the icing.

Position ears and nose on the icing.

Pipe the mouth with writing icing.

Tropical Dinosaurs   p.26

Stir the colour into the buttercream.

Shape the body of the stegosaurus.

Pipe the eyes with white icing.

Farmyard Faces   p.28

Beat until the icing forms stiff peaks.

Place the sheep face on the icing.

Pipe the eyes with writing icing.

Summer Strawberry
Whoopie Pies   p.30

Pipe buttercream on the flat side.

Cut leaves and flowers from icing.

Spread glacé icing on the filled pies.

Wild Animal Cake Pops   p.32

Shape the cake mixture into balls.

Twirl the cake pop in the covering.

Fix the eyes on the cake pop.

 Lucky Bug Whoopie Pies   p.34

 Spread icing with a palette knife.

 Pipe the mouths with writing icing.

 Chocolate discs make great spots.

 Flutterby Butterfly Cakes   p.36

 Dry the butterflies on folded card.

 Cut a shallow circle from the cake.

 Position the icing butterflies.

 Springtime Flowers   p.38

 Beat the butter and cream cheese.

 Cut primroses with a flower cutter.

 Spread a swirl of icing on the cakes.

 Happy Birthday Cupcakes   p.44

 Use a knife to test icing thickness.

 Divide the icing into three and colour.

 Decorate before the icing sets.

 Christmas Cupcakes   p.46

 Beat the egg white until frothy.

 Cut trees with cookie cutters.

 Build a wreath with overlapping discs.

Christmas Tree Cupcakes   p.48

Spread a thin layer of buttercream.

Pipe trees with a star-shaped nozzle.

Position sugar pearls with tweezers.

Snowmen Pops   p.50

Mix the buttercream and crumbs.

Insert a stick into the head and body.

Fix three buttons on the body.

Chinese Dragon   p.52

Insert a strip of icing for the teeth.

Position a scale on each cake.

Pipe lines with writing icing.

Chocolate Nest Cupcakes   p.54

Sift together the flour and cocoa.

Gently mix cornflakes and chocolate.

Make a dip in the middle of the nest.

Flying the Flag Cupcakes   p.56

Add a little milk to the mixture.

Spread icing on the cake.

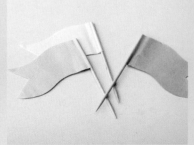

Make flags by gluing strips of paper.

 Fright Night Cupcakes p.58	 Wrap the black icing round the blade.	 Draw veins with a red food pen.	 Place the eyeballs on blobs of jam.
 Pumpkin (Whoopie) Pies p.60	 Smooth the tops with a wet finger.	 Spread filling on the flat side.	 Top each pie with a green stalk.
 Toffee Apple Cupcakes p.62	 Fold in the chopped apple.	 Spread caramel on the cakes.	 Sprinkle over gold stars.
 Well Done! p.66	 Beat until the icing is stiff and glossy.	 Beat in drops of blue colouring.	 Pipe using a large star nozzle.
 Teddy Bears' Picnic Cupcakes p.72	 Weave strips of pink and blue icing.	 Mark eyes with a cocktail stick.	 Pipe grass with a small star nozzle.

Fairy Princess Cupcakes   p.74

Fold in freeze-dried raspberries.

Cut points along one edge.

Fix pearls with a dot of icing.

Sleeping Beauty Towers   p.76

Stick the long sides together.

Spoon icing over top and sides.

Pipe tendrils over the tower.

Pirate Cupcakes   p.78

Cut circles then shape into skulls.

Cut blue circles in half for scarves.

Pipe dots with white icing.

Secret Treasure
Whoopie Pies   p.80

Beat in the cooled white chocolate.

Pipe filling on the flat side.

Sprinkle sweets on one side.

Superhero Cupcakes   p.82

Divide the icing into three and colour.

Cut masks and stars from icing.

Position masks on contrasting icing.

Alien Monster Pops   p.84

Cut scary teeth from white icing.

Twirl the pop in the covering.

Drop on spots of yellow with a stick.

Cars and Trucks Cupcakes   p.88

Add white icing centres to tyres.

Position the vehicle on a cake.

Pipe road lines with white icing.

Magical Sweetshop Cupcakes   p.90

Colour one half of the mixture pink.

Lightly swirl the mixtures together.

Top the icing with a candy cane.

Wizard's Hat Cupcakes   p.92

Shape a quarter into a narrow cone.

Stir melted chocolate into the icing.

Pipe swirls with a large star nozzle.

Queen of Hearts Mini Sandwich Cakes   p.94

Cut hearts with a cookie cutter.

Spread jam on half the cake.

Position the hearts in the centre.

Private Detective Cupcakes   p.96

Wrap black icing round white discs.

Position the footprints – one ahead.

Pipe an outline with writing icing.

Space Explorer Cupcakes   p.98

Fold in the chocolate chips.

Colour the icing dark blue.

Pipe mounds with a large star nozzle.

Ballet Shoes Cupcakes   p.104

Make insoles with white icing.

Overlap the shoes on the icing.

Thin strips of icing make ribbons.

Soccer Fan Cupcakes   p.106

Cut football shirts from icing.

Mark stitching seams with a knife.

Make an American football too.

Summer Holiday Cupcakes p.108

Spread icing over the cakes.

Position coloured sections of the kite.

Position a flag on the sandcastle.

Desert Island Cupcakes   p.110

Add banana, pineapple and orange rind.

Swirl blue icing on the cakes.

Pipe wave tops with writing icing.

White Chocolate and
Raspberry Cones   p.112

Divide mixture between the cones.

Beat purée into the buttercream.

Sprinkle with raspberry pieces.

Mix and Match Cupcakes p.114

Cut clothes and bodies from icing.

Position pieces on the cakes.

Mark features on the faces.

Mini Macaron Lollipops   p.116

Sprinkle decorations before cooking.

Remove from the paper with a knife.

Spread buttercream on the flat side.

Rainbow Magic Cupcakes p.120

Lightly swirl the mixtures together.

Spoon alternate colours into the bag.

Pipe mounds of mixed colour.

Jewels and Gems Cupcakes   p.122   Spread icing on the cupcakes.   Arrange decorations on the piping.   Brush piping with edible gold paint.

Perfect Purple Cupcakes   p.128   Gently fold in the berries.   Stir colouring into the buttercream.   Decorate with a few blueberries.

Chocolate Explosion Cupcakes   p.130   Insert squares of chocolate.   Pipe a shallow swirl of buttercream.   Decorate with chocolates.

Honeybee Cupcakes   p.132   Add a little milk to the mixture.   Wrap strips of icing round the bodies.   Position the bees on the hive.

White Chocolate and Raspberry Cake Pops   p.134   Beat in the raspberry jam.   Twirl the pop in the chocolate.   Decorate before the chocolate sets.

Marshmallow Mint
Chocolate Whoopie Pies   p.136

Transfer the pies with a palette knife.

Fold in the marshmallow fluff.

Spread icing on the filled pie.

Lemon and Raisin
Cupcakes   p.138

Test the bounciness of the cakes.

Spread icing on the cake.

Decorate before the icing sets.

Strawberries and
Cream Cupcakes   p.140

Put a spoonful of jam in the middle.

Pipe cream with a large star nozzle.

Position slices of strawberry on top.

Coconut Ice Cupcakes   p.142

Alternate coloured mixture.

Shake coconut with colouring in a jar.

Sprinkle coloured coconut on top.

Maple Syrup Cupcakes   p.144

Fold in the chopped nuts.

Cut leaves with a cookie cutter.

Position leaves on the top.

For all our family and loved ones.

This edition is published by Lorenz Books, an imprint of Anness Publishing Ltd,
108 Great Russell Street, London WC1B 3NA; info@anness.com

www.lorenzbooks.com; www.annesspublishing.com

If you like the images in this book and would like to investigate using them
for publishing, promotions or advertising, please visit our website
www.practicalpictures.com for more information.

A CIP catalogue record for this book is available from the British Library.

Publisher: Joanna Lorenz
Studio photography: William Lingwood
Food stylist: Lucy McElvie
Prop stylist: Lisa Harrison
Location photography: Josie Ainscough
Designer: Jane McKenna

With special thanks to the models: Cressida, Bella, Maia, Holly, Freddie, Sam and Peter

NOTES
Bracketed terms are intended for American readers.
For all recipes, quantities are given in both metric and imperial measures and, where appropriate,
in standard cups and spoons. Follow one set of measures, but not a mixture, because they
are not interchangeable.
Standard spoon and cup measures are level. 1 tsp = 5ml, 1 tbsp = 15ml, 1 cup = 250ml/8fl oz.
Australian standard tablespoons are 20ml. Australian readers should use 3 tsp in place of 1 tbsp
for measuring small quantities.
American pints are 16fl oz/2 cups. American readers should use 20fl oz/2.5 cups in place of 1 pint
when measuring liquids.
Electric oven temperatures in this book are for conventional ovens. When using a fan oven,
the temperature will probably need to be reduced by about 10–20°C/20–40°F. Since ovens vary,
you should check with your manufacturer's instruction book for guidance.
The nutritional analysis given for each recipe is calculated per portion (i.e. serving or item), unless
otherwise stated. If the recipe gives a range, such as Serves 4–6, then the nutritional analysis will be
for the smaller portion size, i.e. 6 servings. The analysis does not include optional ingredients, such
as salt added to taste.
Medium (US large) eggs are used unless otherwise stated.
Unsalted (sweet) butter has generally been used.

PUBLISHER'S NOTE
Although the advice and information in this book are believed to be accurate and true at the time of going
to press, neither the authors nor the publisher can accept any legal responsibility or liability for any errors
or omissions that may have been made nor for any inaccuracies nor for any loss, harm or injury that comes
about from following instructions or advice in this book.